GRAPHIC SCIENCE

UNDERSTANDING

VIRUSES

WITH MAX AXIOM
SUPER SCIENTIST

by Agnieszka Biskup

illustrated by Nick Derington

Consultant:

Wade A. Bresnahan, PhD
Associate Professor
Department of Microbiology
University of Minnesota

Capstone
press®

Mankato, Minnesota

Graphic Library is published by Capstone Press,
151 Good Counsel Drive, P.O. Box 669, Mankato, Minnesota 56002.
www.capstonepress.com

Printed in the United States of America in Stevens Point, Wisconsin.
122009
005651R

Library of Congress Cataloging-in-Publication Data
Biskup, Agnieszka.
    Understanding viruses with Max Axiom, super scientist / by Agnieszka Biskup;
illustrated by Nick Derington.
       p. cm. — (Graphic library. Graphic science)
    Includes bibliographical references and index.
    Summary: "In graphic novel format, follows the adventures of Max Axiom as he
explains the science behind viruses" — Provided by publisher.
    ISBN-13: 978-1-4296-2338-4 (hardcover)
    ISBN-10: 1-4296-2338-1 (hardcover)
    ISBN-13: 978-1-4296-3453-3 (softcover pbk.)
    ISBN-10: 1-4296-3453-7 (softcover pbk.)
    1. Viruses — Juvenile literature. 2. Virus diseases — Juvenile literature. I. Derington,
Nick, ill. II. Title.
QR365.B57 2009
579.2 — dc22   2008029654

Set Designer
Bob Lentz

Book Designer
Alison Thiele

Cover Artist
Tod G. Smith

Editor
Christopher L. Harbo

Photo illustration credits: iStockphoto/Tony Sanchez, 13

TABLE OF CONTENTS

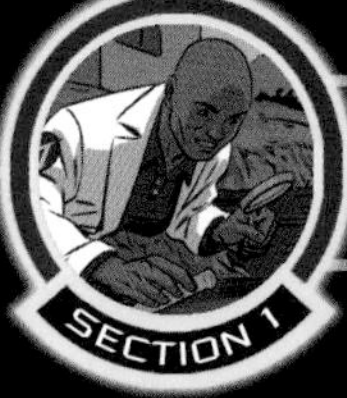
SECTION 1

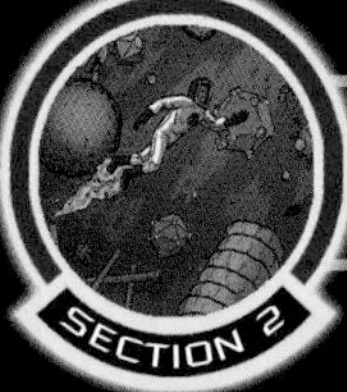
SECTION 2

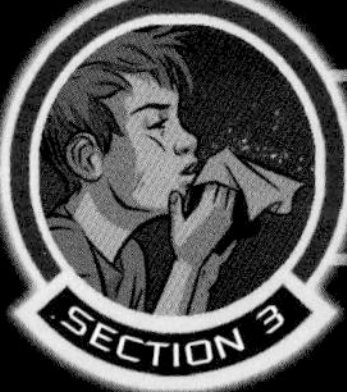
SECTION 3

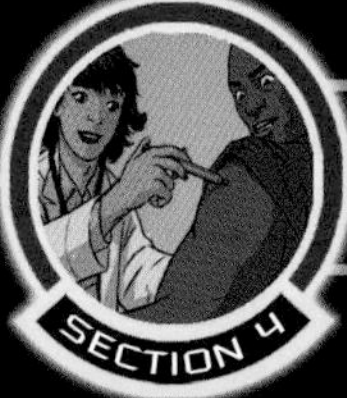
SECTION 4

SECTION 1 A MICROSCOPIC WORLD

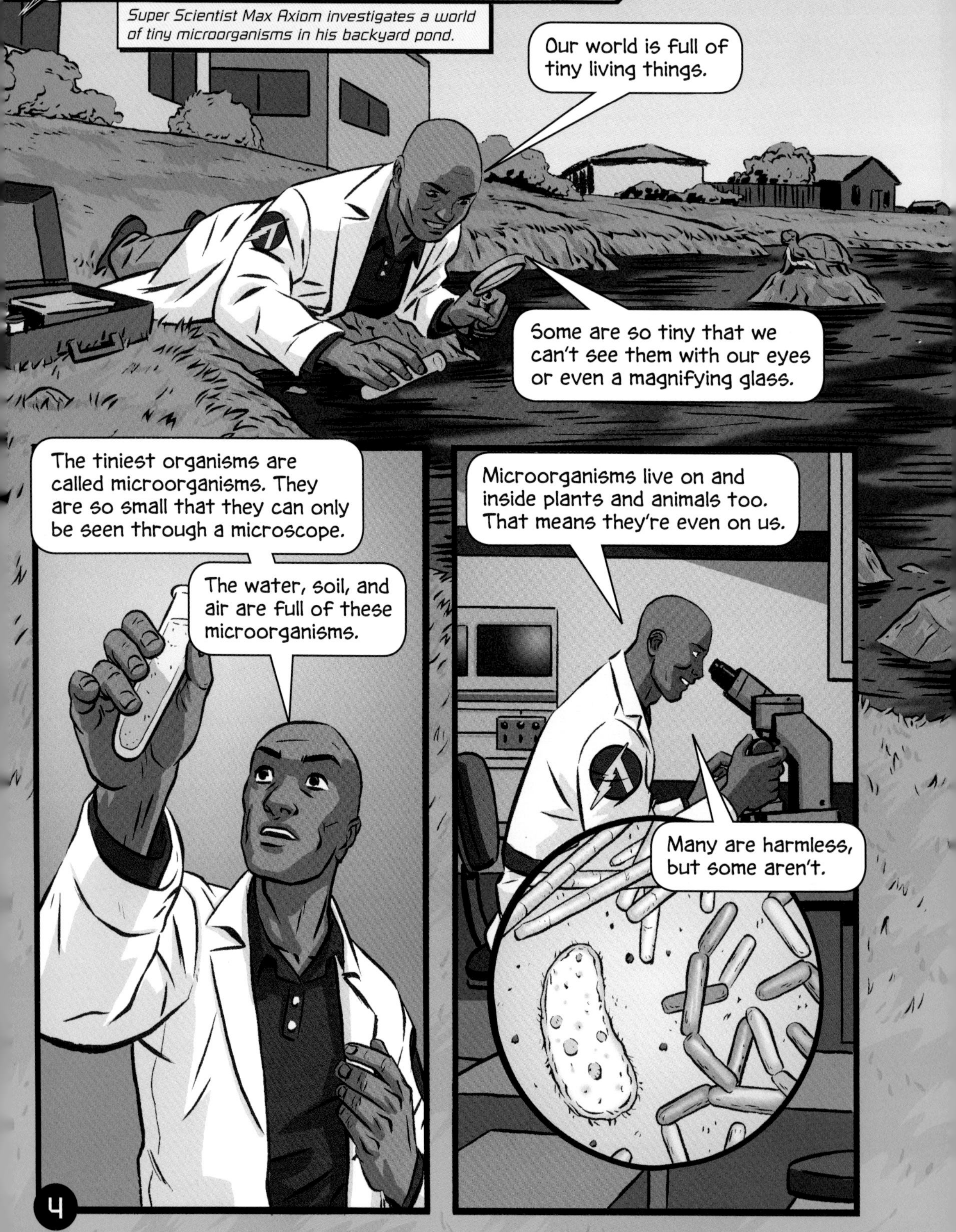
Super Scientist Max Axiom investigates a world of tiny microorganisms in his backyard pond.
Our world is full of tiny living things.
Some are so tiny that we can't see them with our eyes or even a magnifying glass.
The tiniest organisms are called microorganisms. They are so small that they can only be seen through a microscope.
The water, soil, and air are full of these microorganisms.
Microorganisms live on and inside plants and animals too. That means they're even on us.
Many are harmless, but some aren't.

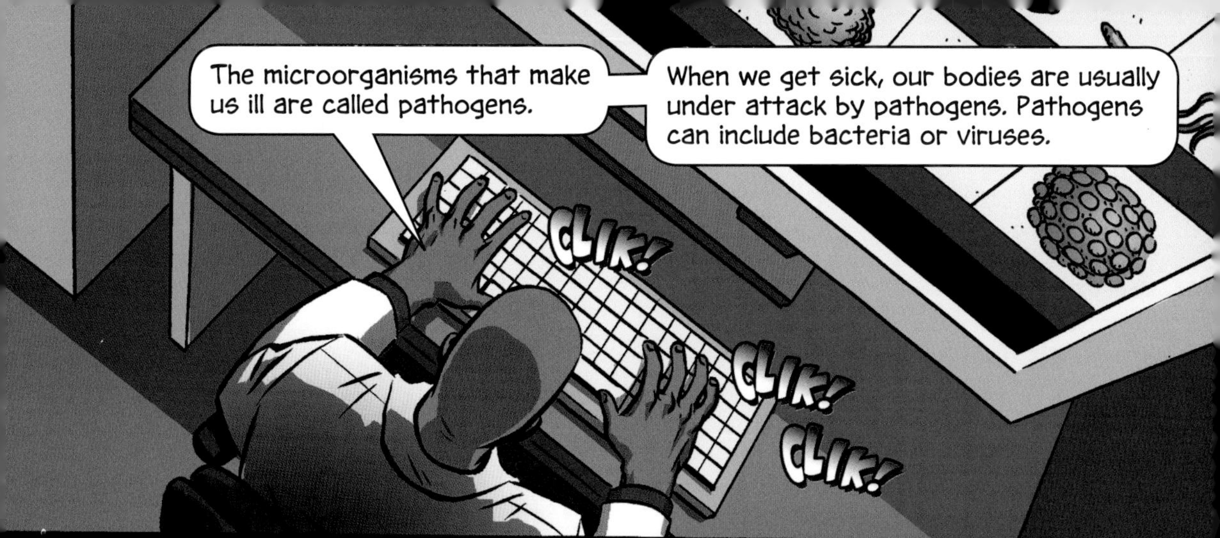
The microorganisms that make us ill are called pathogens.
When we get sick, our bodies are usually under attack by pathogens. Pathogens can include bacteria or viruses.
CLIK!
CLIK!
CLIK!

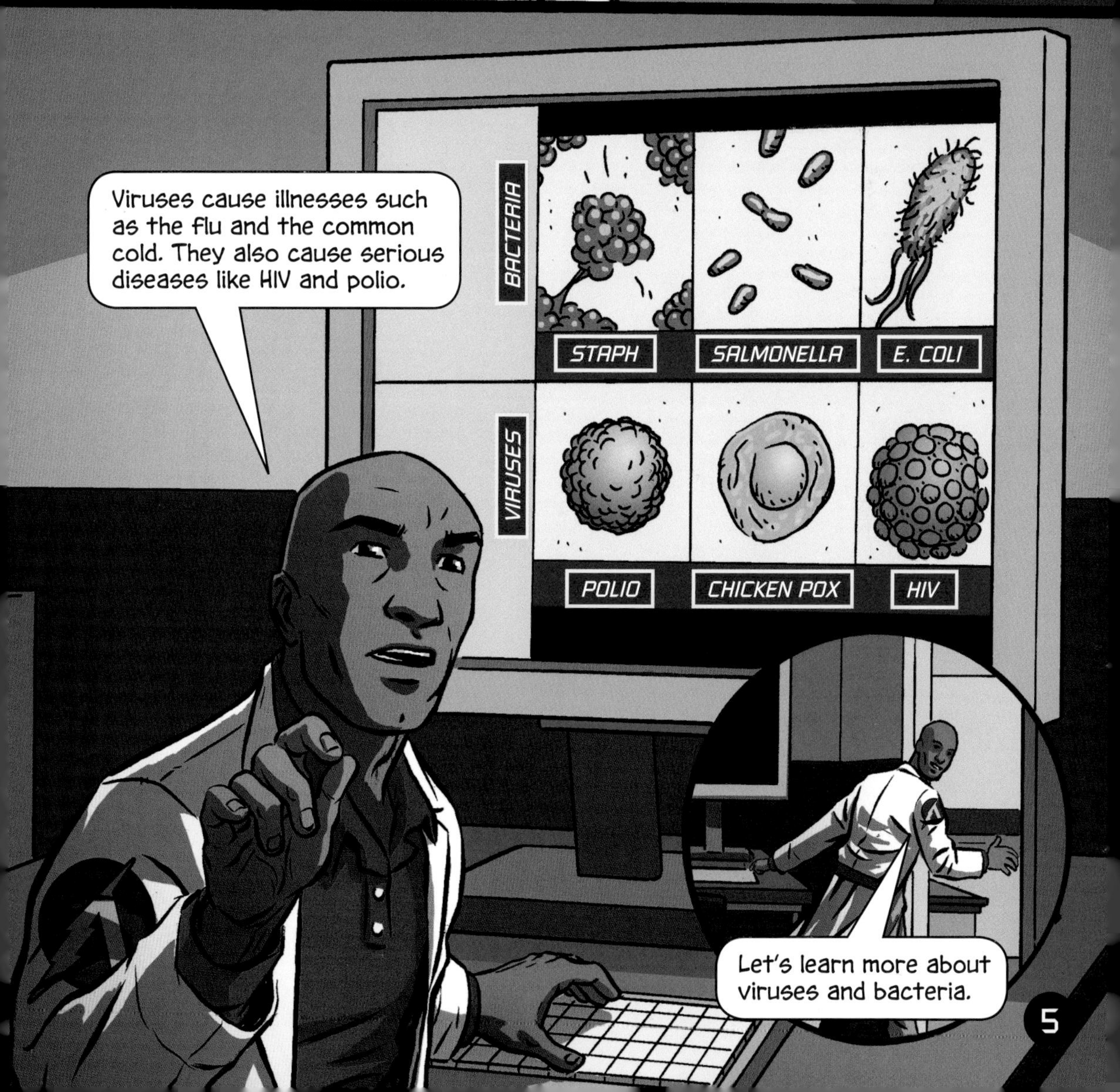
Viruses cause illnesses such as the flu and the common cold. They also cause serious diseases like HIV and polio.
BACTERIA
STAPH
SALMONELLA
E. COLI
VIRUSES
POLIO
CHICKEN POX
HIV
Let's learn more about viruses and bacteria.

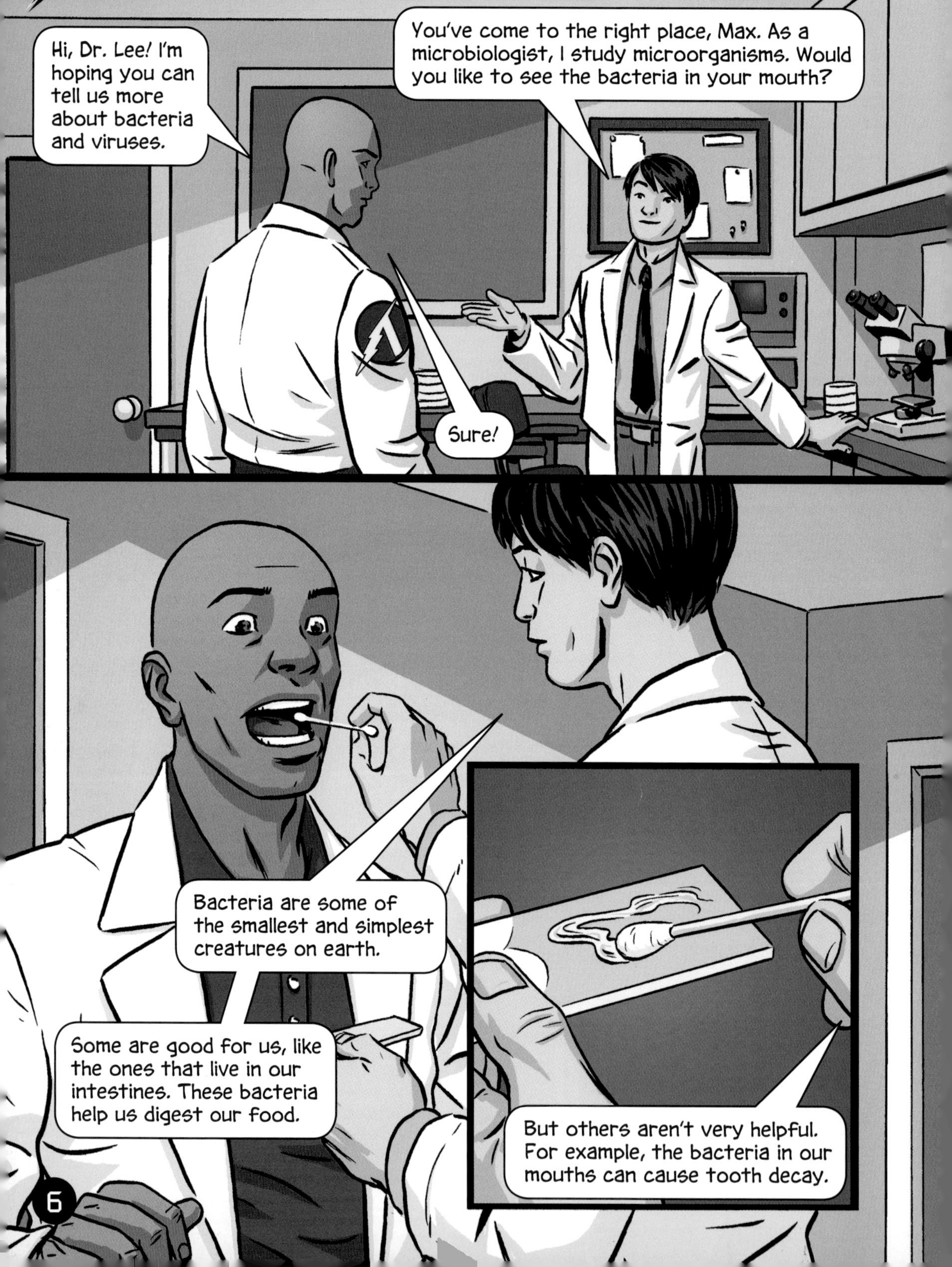
Hi, Dr. Lee! I'm hoping you can tell us more about bacteria and viruses.
You've come to the right place, Max. As a microbiologist, I study microorganisms. Would you like to see the bacteria in your mouth?
Sure!
Bacteria are some of the smallest and simplest creatures on earth.
Some are good for us, like the ones that live in our intestines. These bacteria help us digest our food.
But others aren't very helpful. For example, the bacteria in our mouths can cause tooth decay.

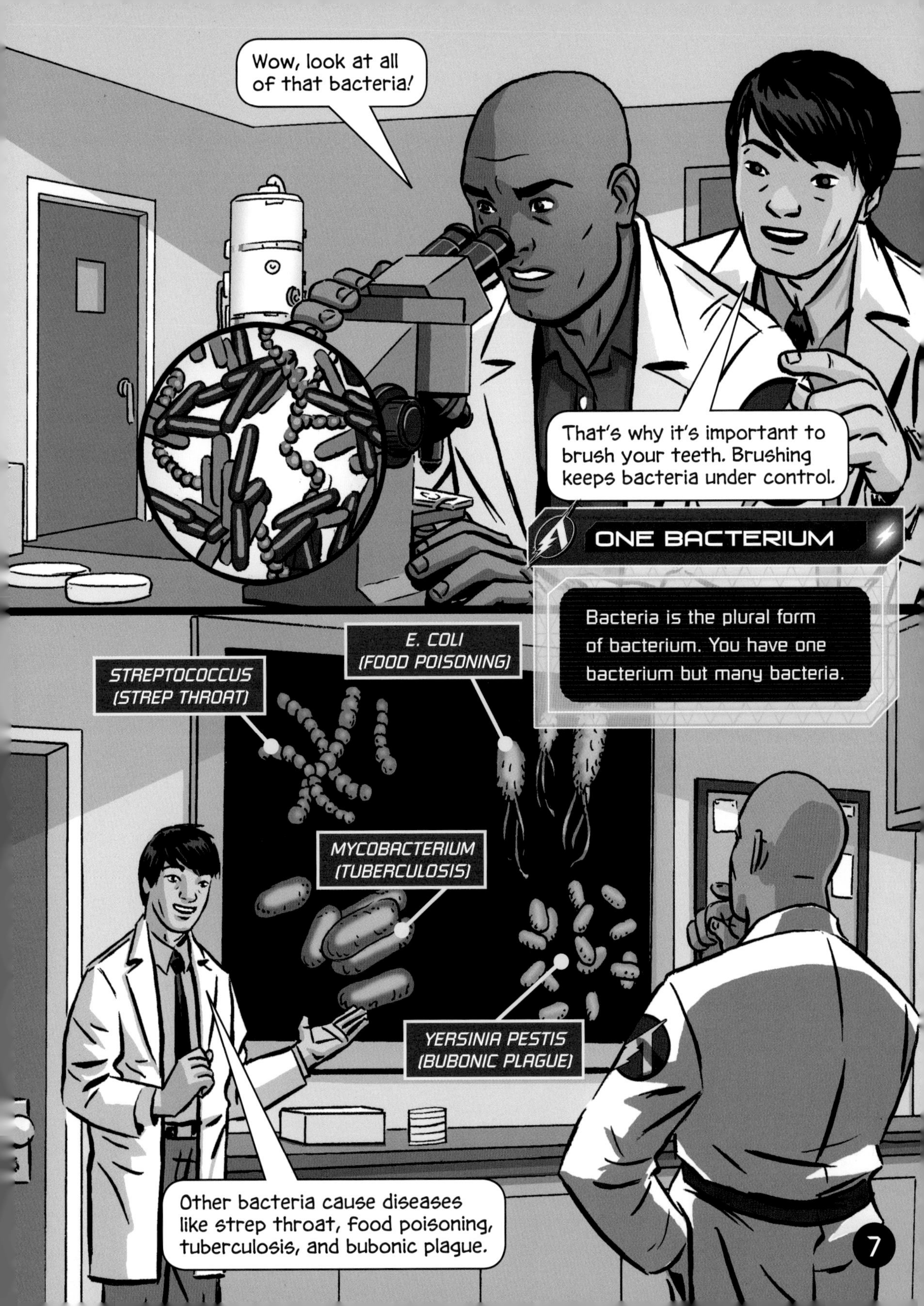

Wow, look at all of that bacteria!
That's why it's important to brush your teeth. Brushing keeps bacteria under control.
ONE BACTERIUM
Bacteria is the plural form of bacterium. You have one bacterium but many bacteria.
STREPTOCOCCUS (STREP THROAT)
E. COLI (FOOD POISONING)
MYCOBACTERIUM (TUBERCULOSIS)
YERSINIA PESTIS (BUBONIC PLAGUE)
Other bacteria cause diseases like strep throat, food poisoning, tuberculosis, and bubonic plague.

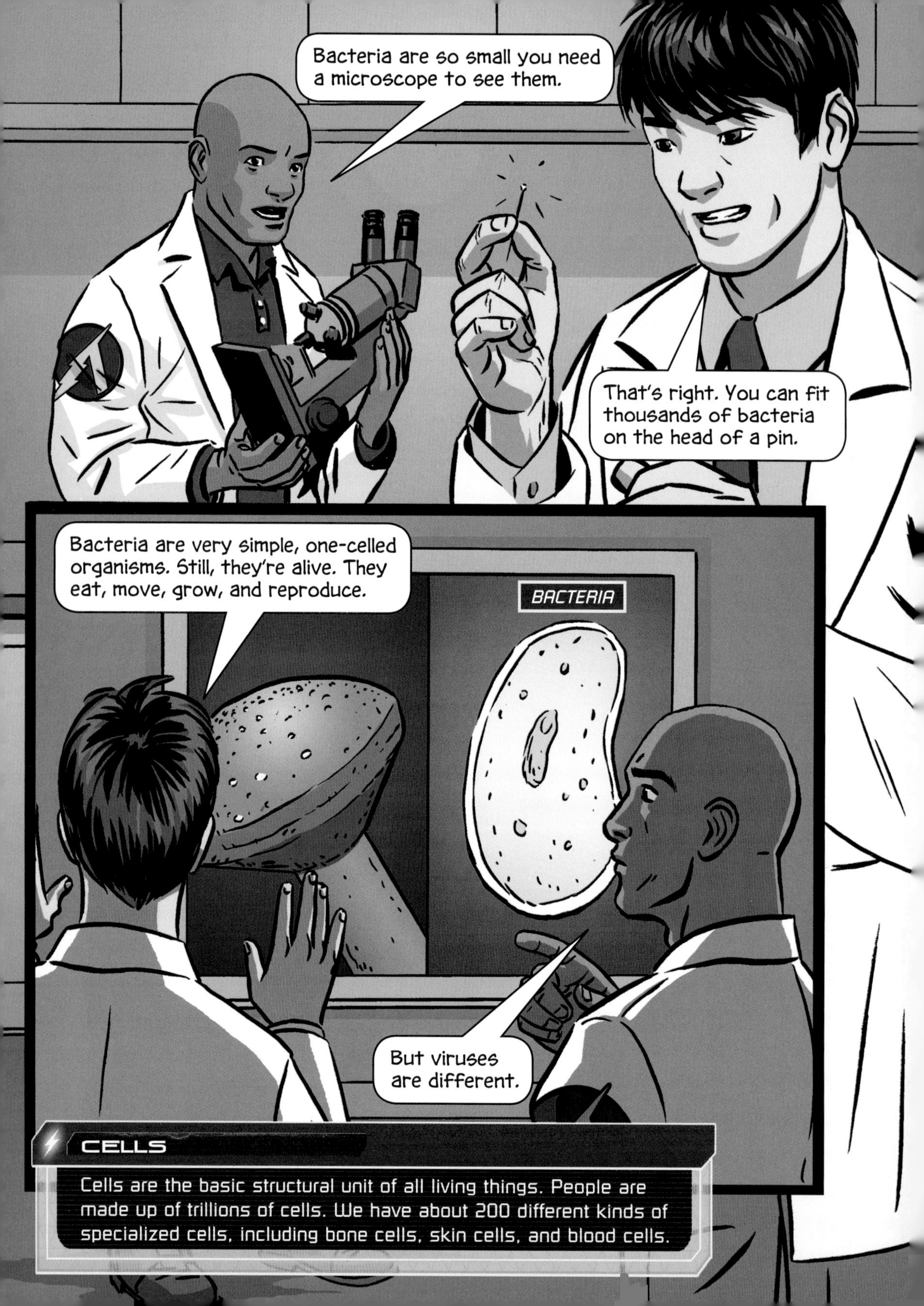
Bacteria are so small you need a microscope to see them.
That's right. You can fit thousands of bacteria on the head of a pin.
Bacteria are very simple, one-celled organisms. Still, they're alive. They eat, move, grow, and reproduce.
BACTERIA
But viruses are different.
CELLS
Cells are the basic structural unit of all living things. People are made up of trillions of cells. We have about 200 different kinds of specialized cells, including bone cells, skin cells, and blood cells.

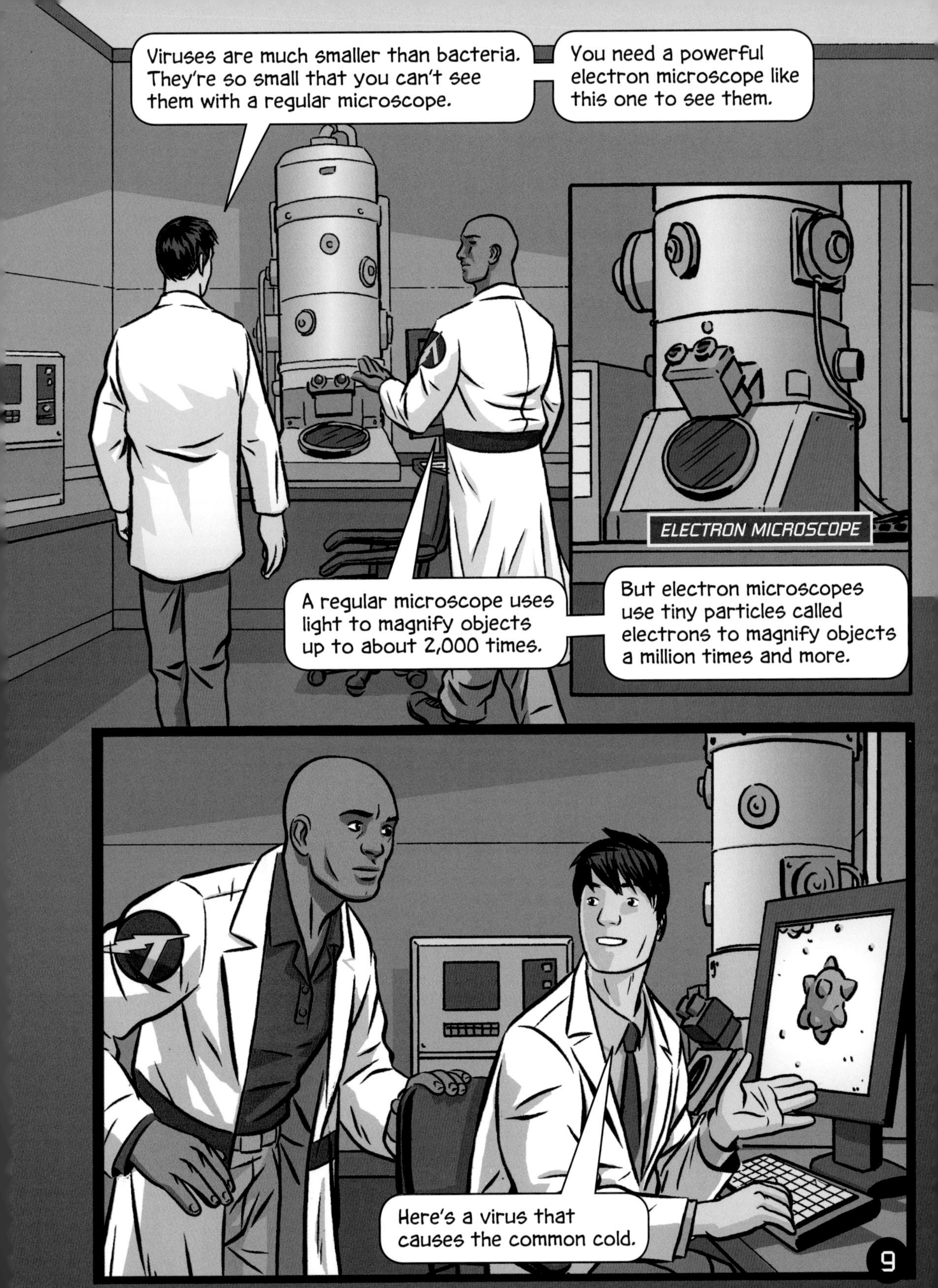
Viruses are much smaller than bacteria. They're so small that you can't see them with a regular microscope.
You need a powerful electron microscope like this one to see them.
ELECTRON MICROSCOPE
A regular microscope uses light to magnify objects up to about 2,000 times.
But electron microscopes use tiny particles called electrons to magnify objects a million times and more.
Here's a virus that causes the common cold.

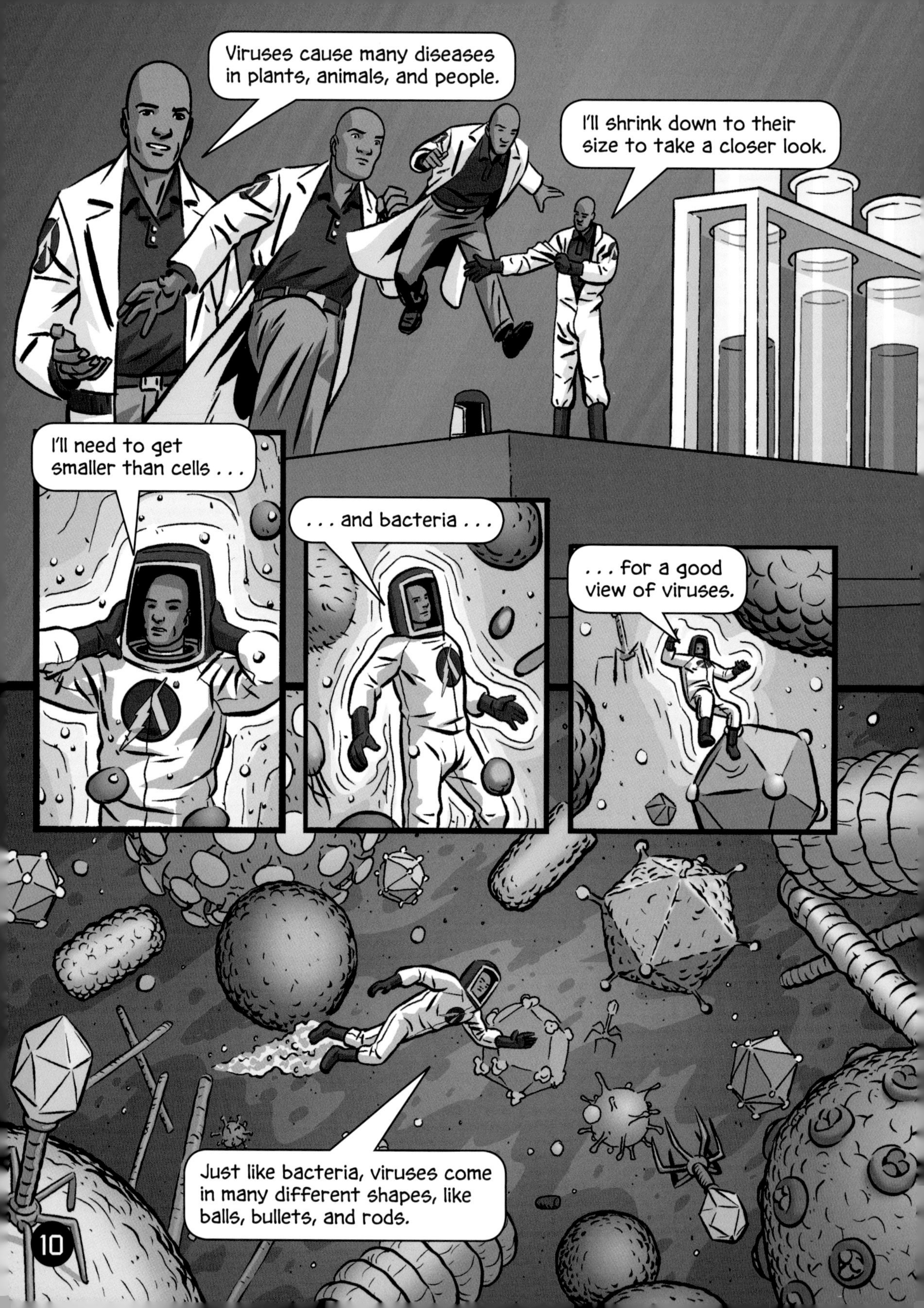
Viruses cause many diseases in plants, animals, and people.
I'll shrink down to their size to take a closer look.
I'll need to get smaller than cells . . .
. . . and bacteria . . .
. . . for a good view of viruses.
Just like bacteria, viruses come in many different shapes, like balls, bullets, and rods.

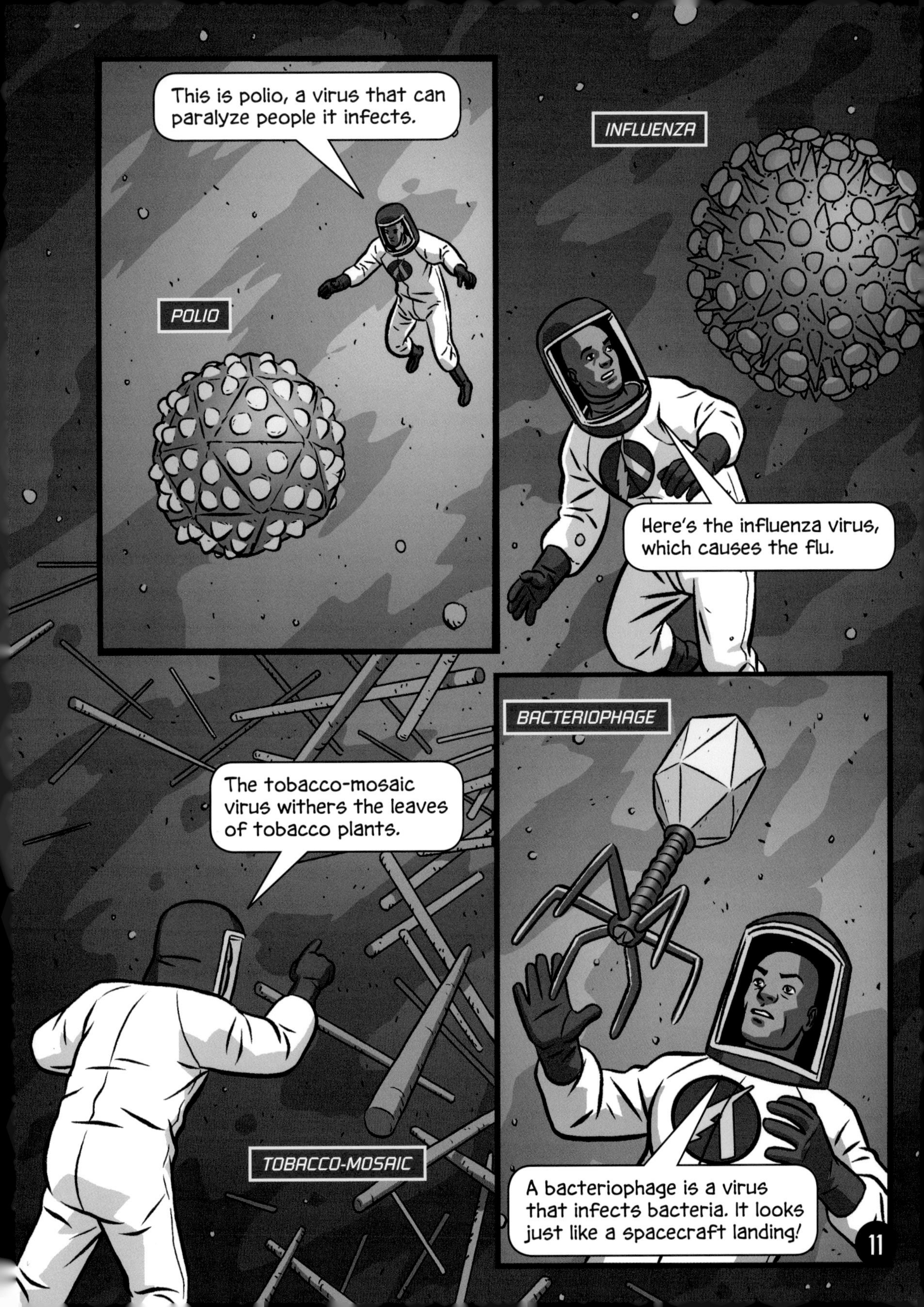
This is polio, a virus that can paralyze people it infects.
POLIO
INFLUENZA
Here's the influenza virus, which causes the flu.
The tobacco-mosaic virus withers the leaves of tobacco plants.
TOBACCO-MOSAIC
BACTERIOPHAGE
A bacteriophage is a virus that infects bacteria. It looks just like a spacecraft landing!

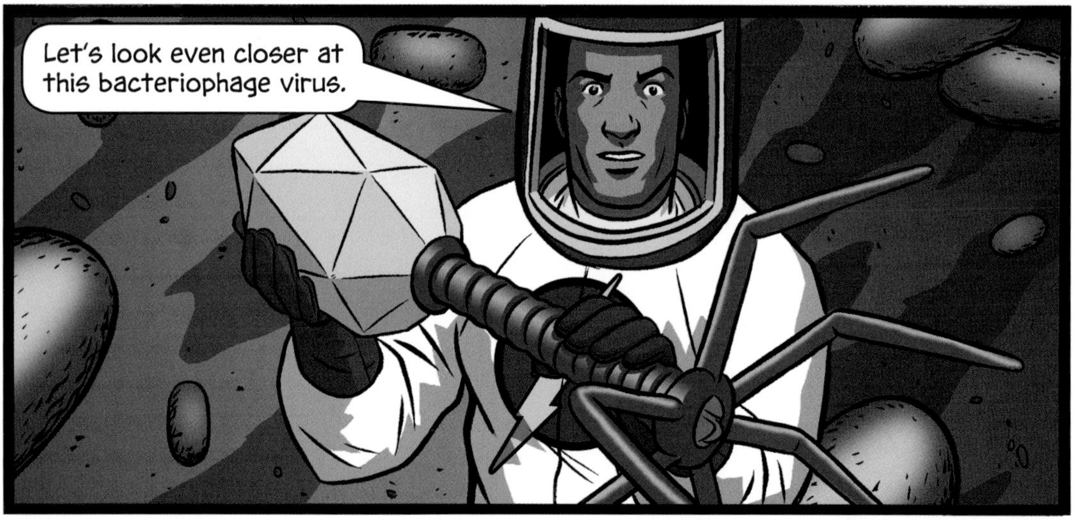
Let's look even closer at this bacteriophage virus.

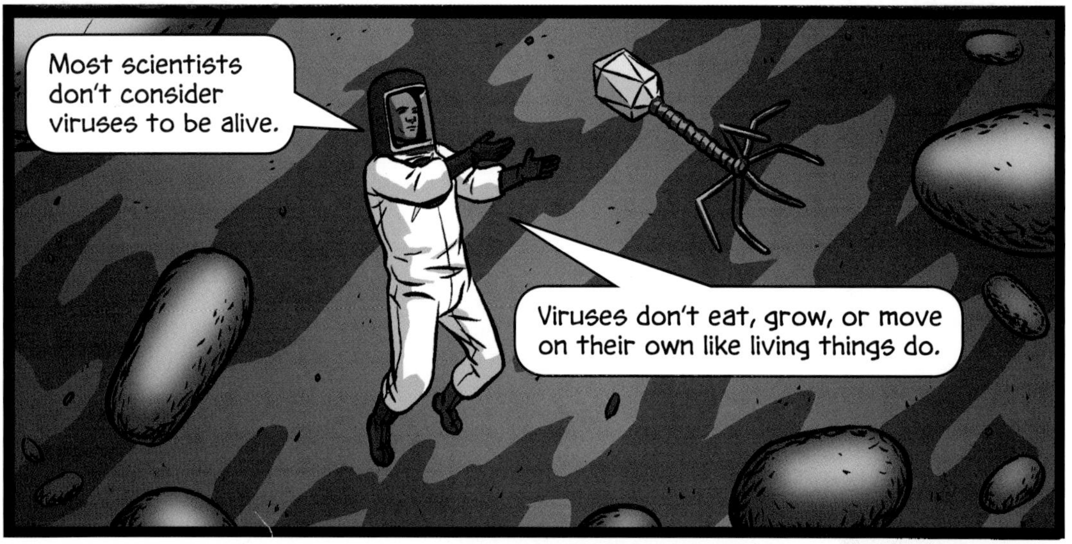
Most scientists don't consider viruses to be alive.
Viruses don't eat, grow, or move on their own like living things do.

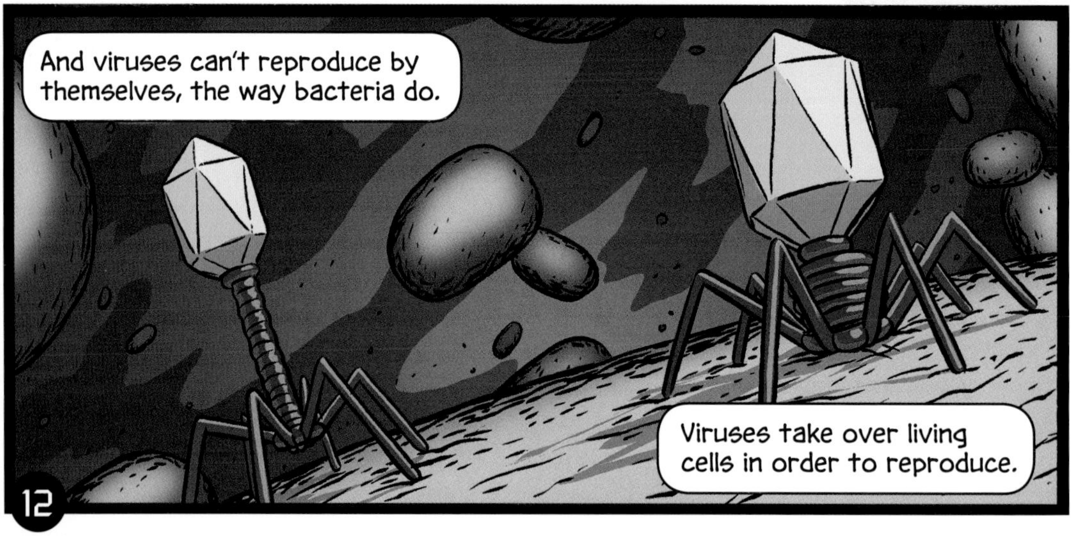
And viruses can't reproduce by themselves, the way bacteria do.
Viruses take over living cells in order to reproduce.

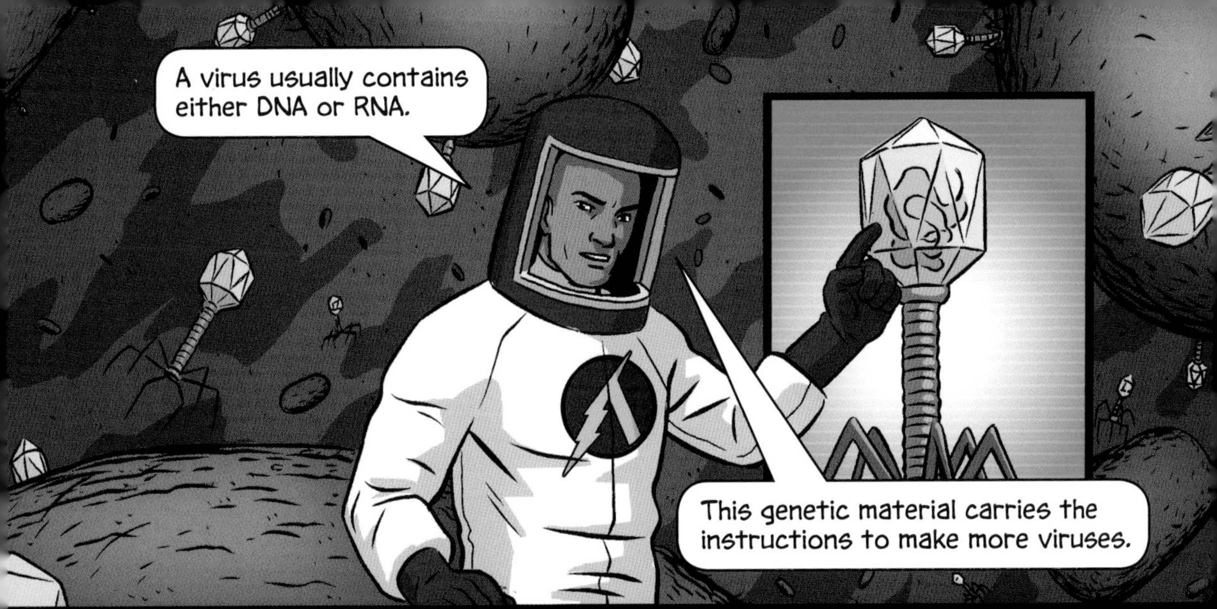
A virus usually contains either DNA or RNA.
This genetic material carries the instructions to make more viruses.

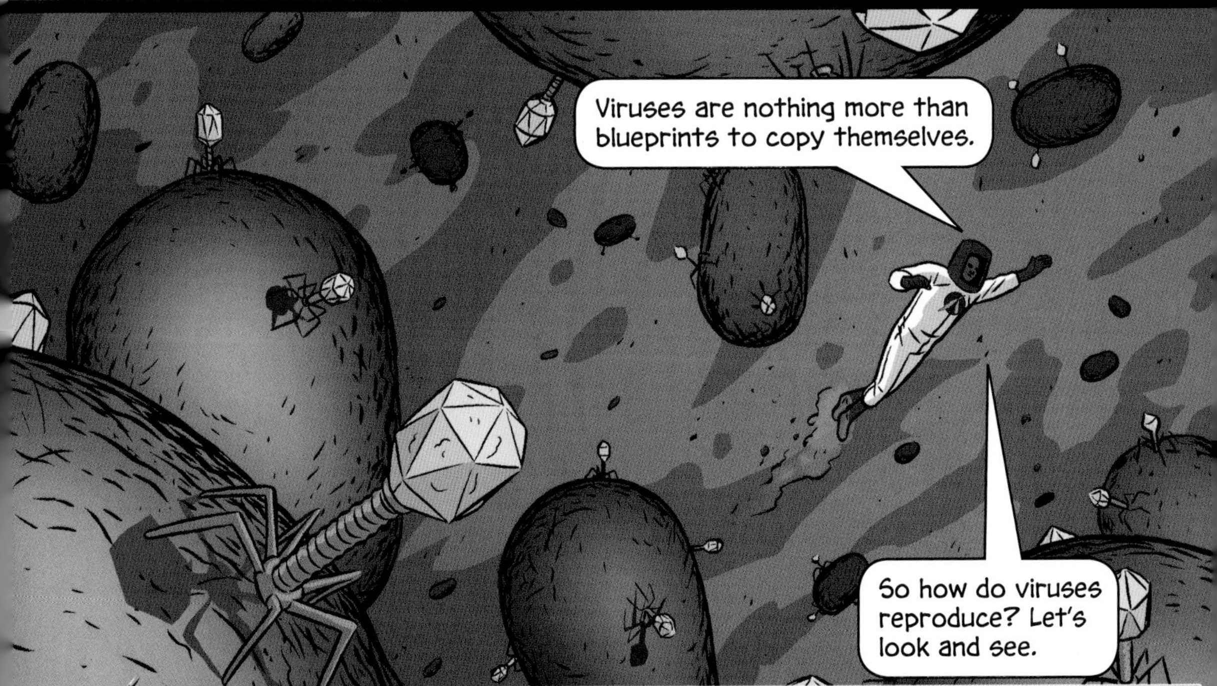
Viruses are nothing more than blueprints to copy themselves.
So how do viruses reproduce? Let's look and see.

DNA AND RNA

ACCESS GRANTED: MAX AXIOM

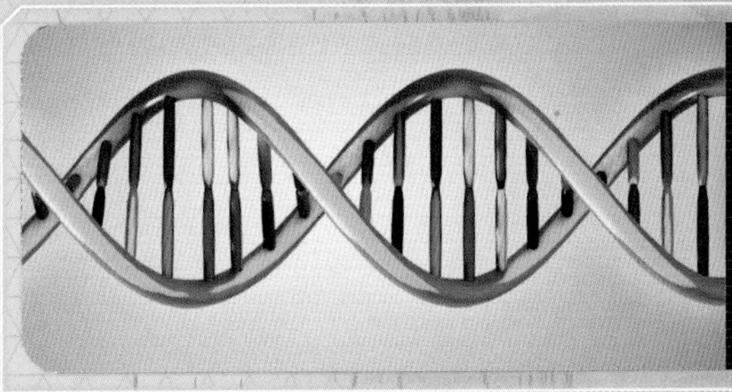

All living cells contain DNA and RNA. DNA provides all the instructions to operate and copy the cell. Cells use RNA to help translate DNA's instructions.

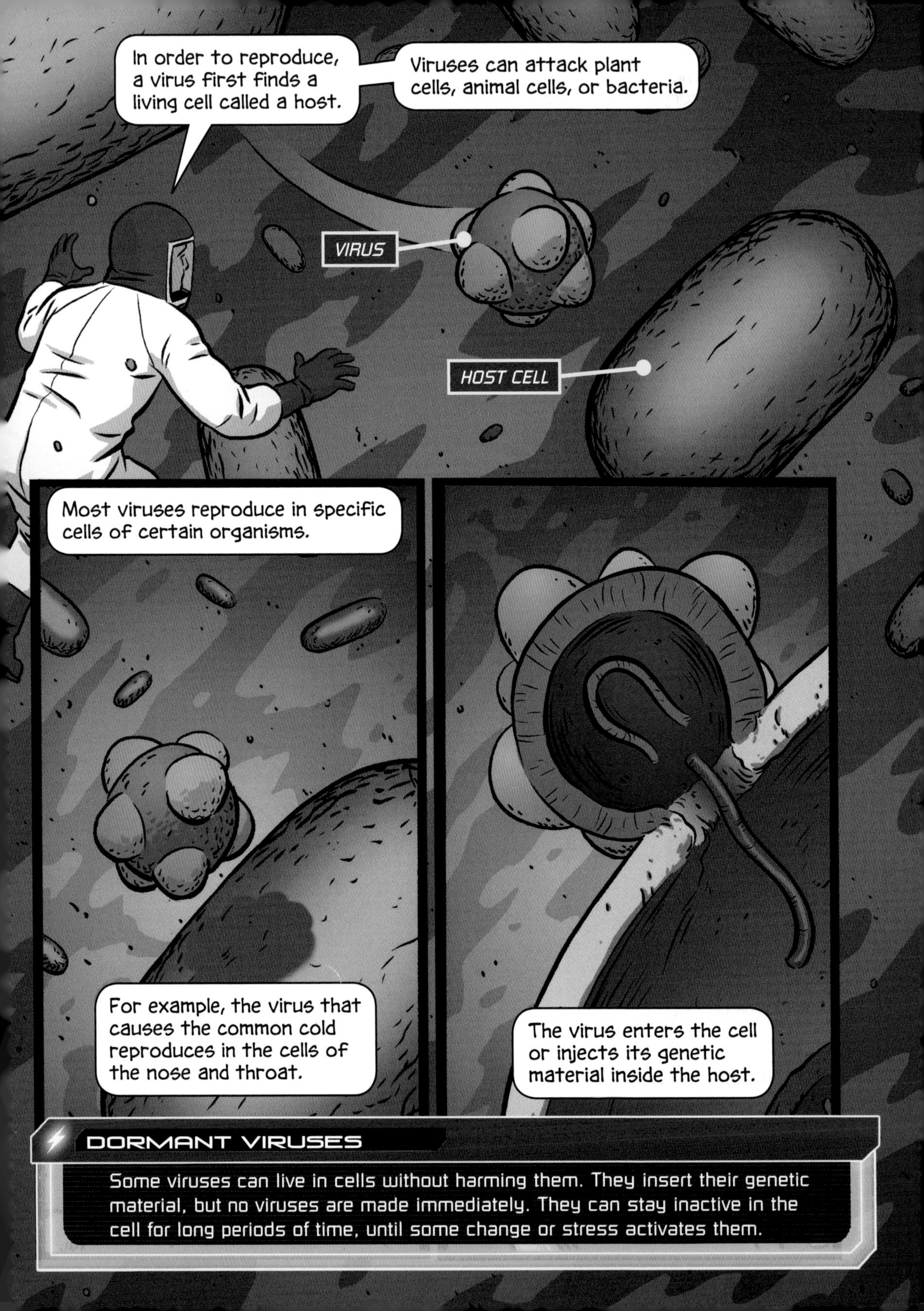
In order to reproduce, a virus first finds a living cell called a host.
Viruses can attack plant cells, animal cells, or bacteria.
VIRUS
HOST CELL
Most viruses reproduce in specific cells of certain organisms.
For example, the virus that causes the common cold reproduces in the cells of the nose and throat.
The virus enters the cell or injects its genetic material inside the host.

DORMANT VIRUSES

Some viruses can live in cells without harming them. They insert their genetic material, but no viruses are made immediately. They can stay inactive in the cell for long periods of time, until some change or stress activates them.

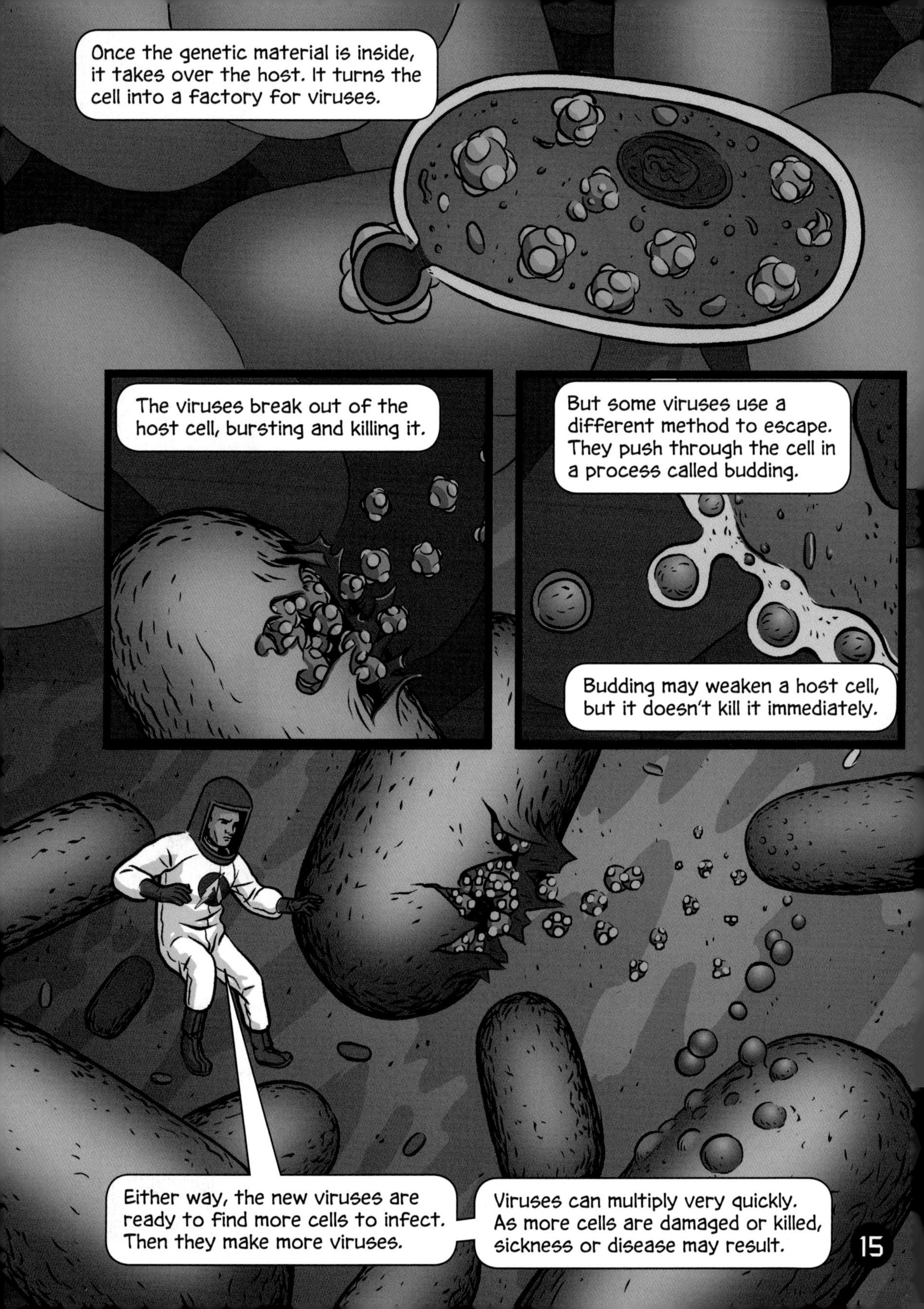
Once the genetic material is inside, it takes over the host. It turns the cell into a factory for viruses.
The viruses break out of the host cell, bursting and killing it.
But some viruses use a different method to escape. They push through the cell in a process called budding.
Budding may weaken a host cell, but it doesn't kill it immediately.
Either way, the new viruses are ready to find more cells to infect. Then they make more viruses.
Viruses can multiply very quickly. As more cells are damaged or killed, sickness or disease may result.

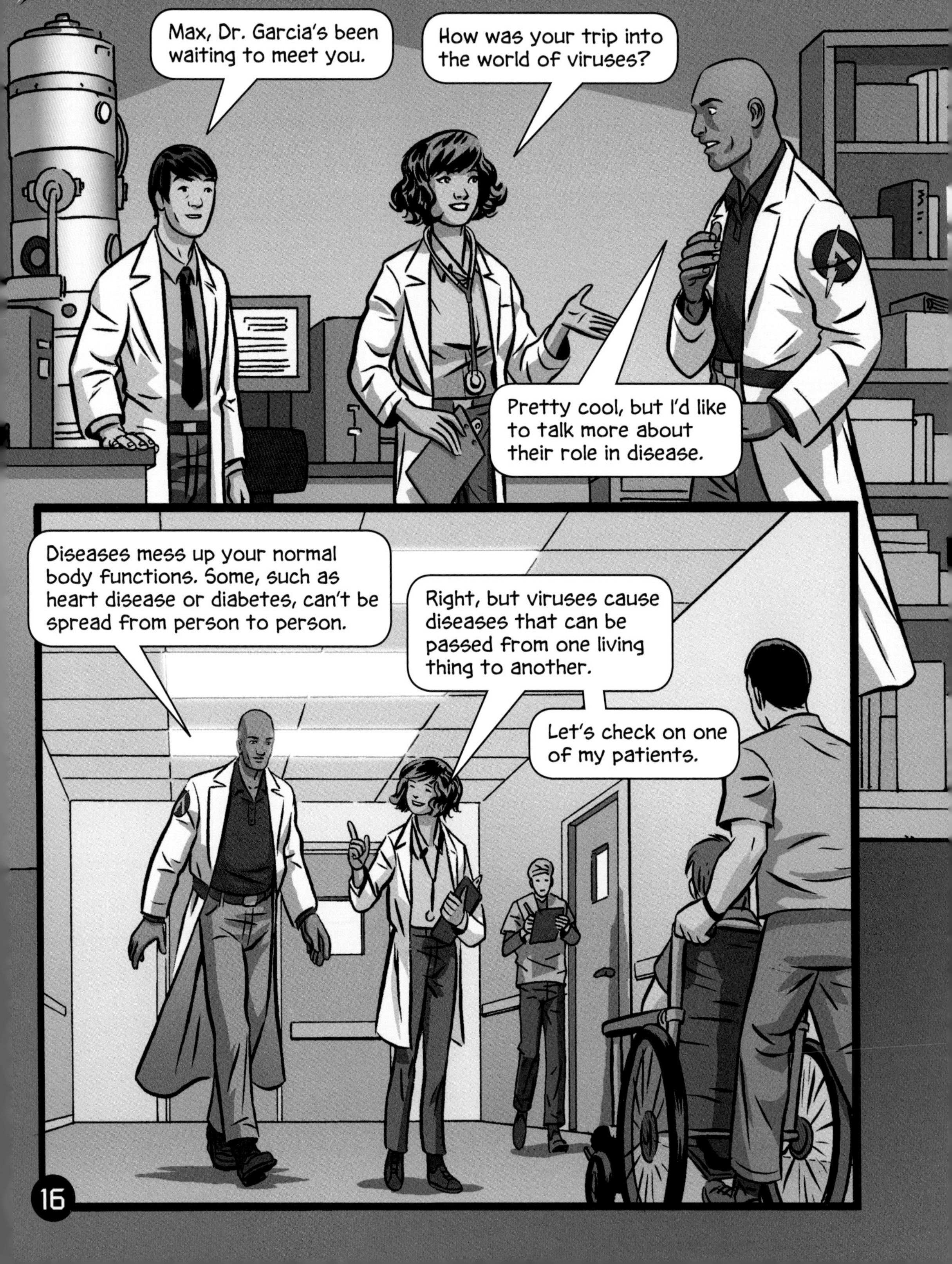
Max, Dr. Garcia's been waiting to meet you.
How was your trip into the world of viruses?
Pretty cool, but I'd like to talk more about their role in disease.
Diseases mess up your normal body functions. Some, such as heart disease or diabetes, can't be spread from person to person.
Right, but viruses cause diseases that can be passed from one living thing to another.
Let's check on one of my patients.

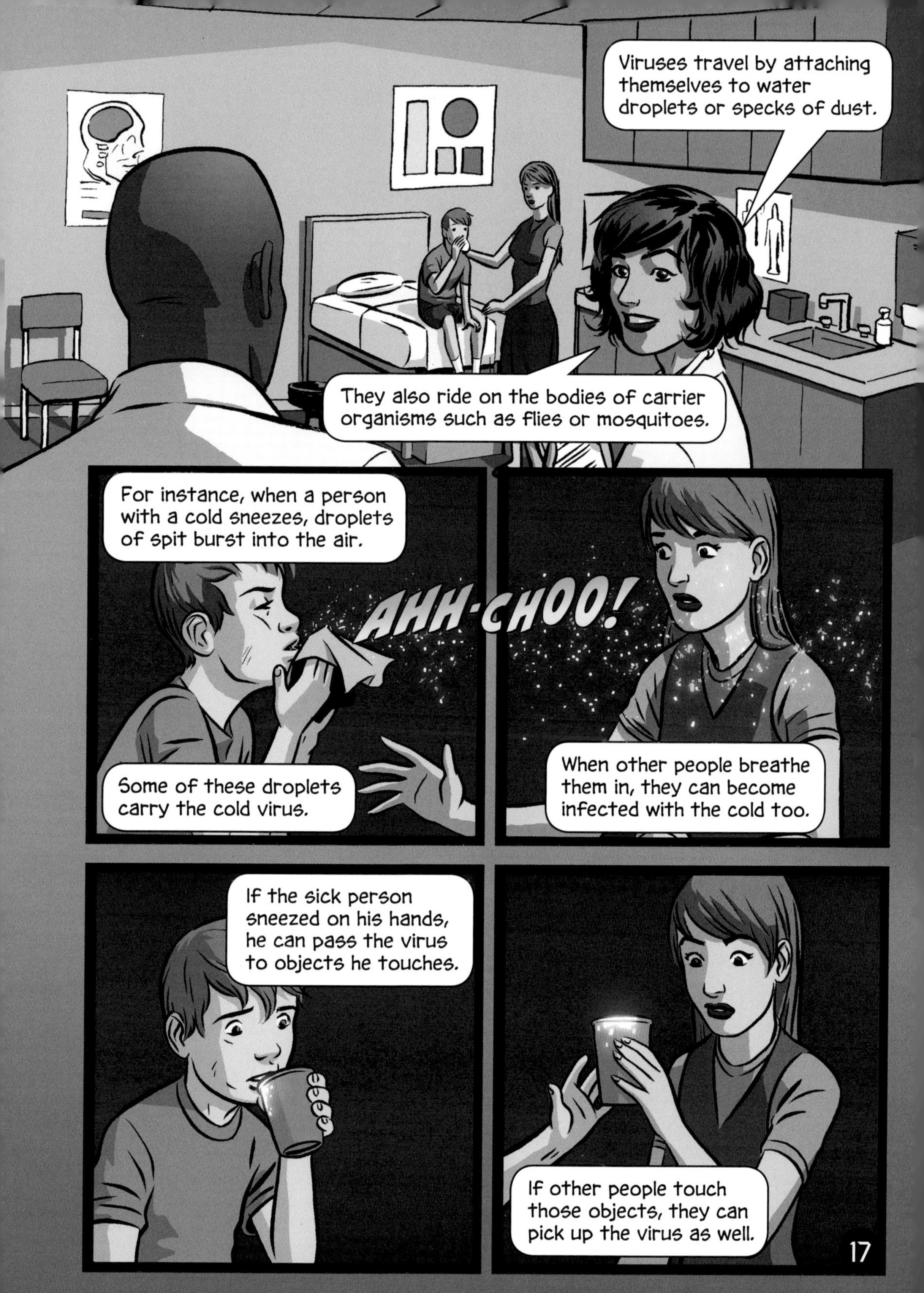
Viruses travel by attaching themselves to water droplets or specks of dust.
They also ride on the bodies of carrier organisms such as flies or mosquitoes.
For instance, when a person with a cold sneezes, droplets of spit burst into the air.
AHH-CHOO!
Some of these droplets carry the cold virus.
When other people breathe them in, they can become infected with the cold too.
If the sick person sneezed on his hands, he can pass the virus to objects he touches.
If other people touch those objects, they can pick up the virus as well.

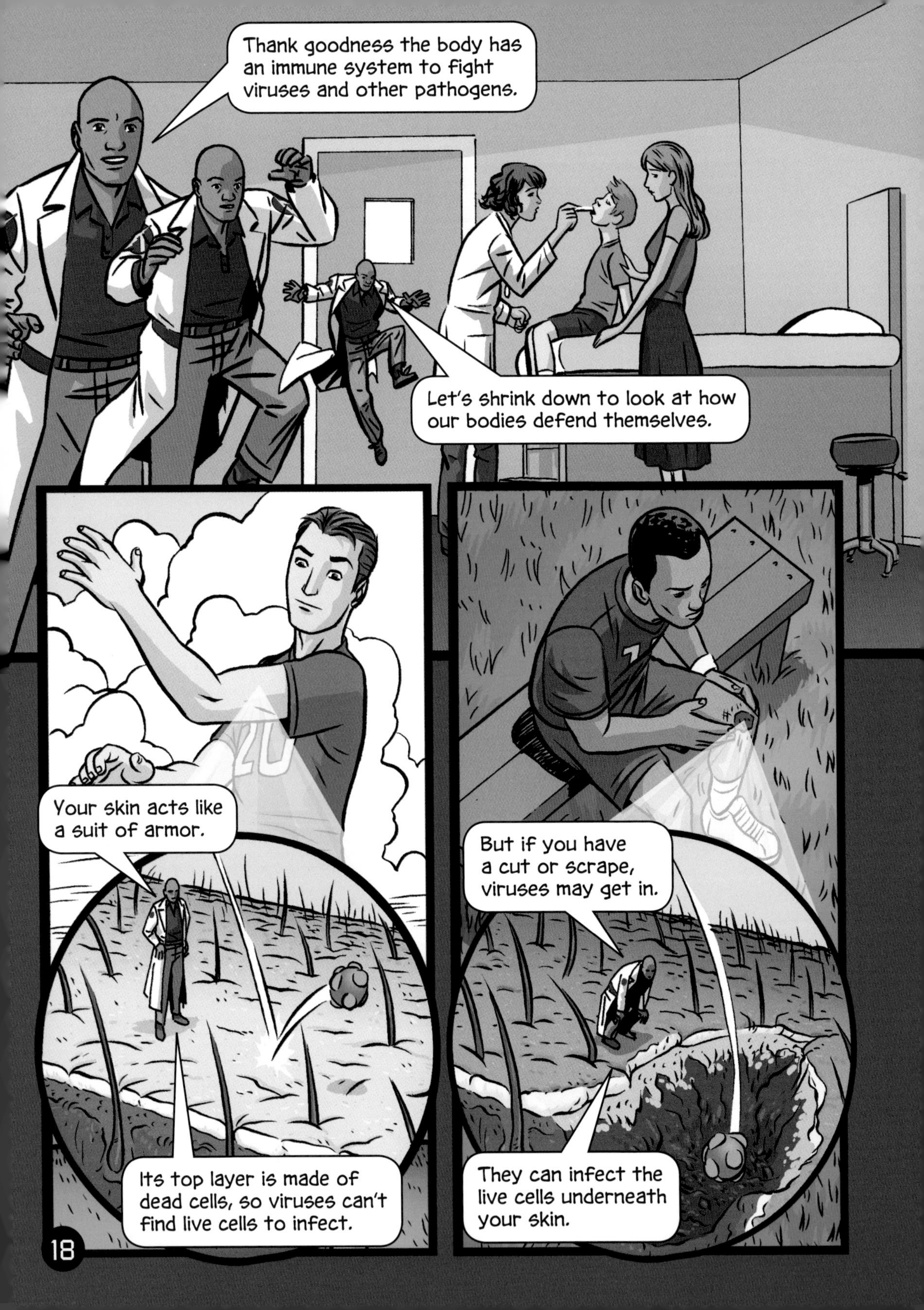

Thank goodness the body has an immune system to fight viruses and other pathogens.
Let's shrink down to look at how our bodies defend themselves.
Your skin acts like a suit of armor.
Its top layer is made of dead cells, so viruses can't find live cells to infect.
But if you have a cut or scrape, viruses may get in.
They can infect the live cells underneath your skin.

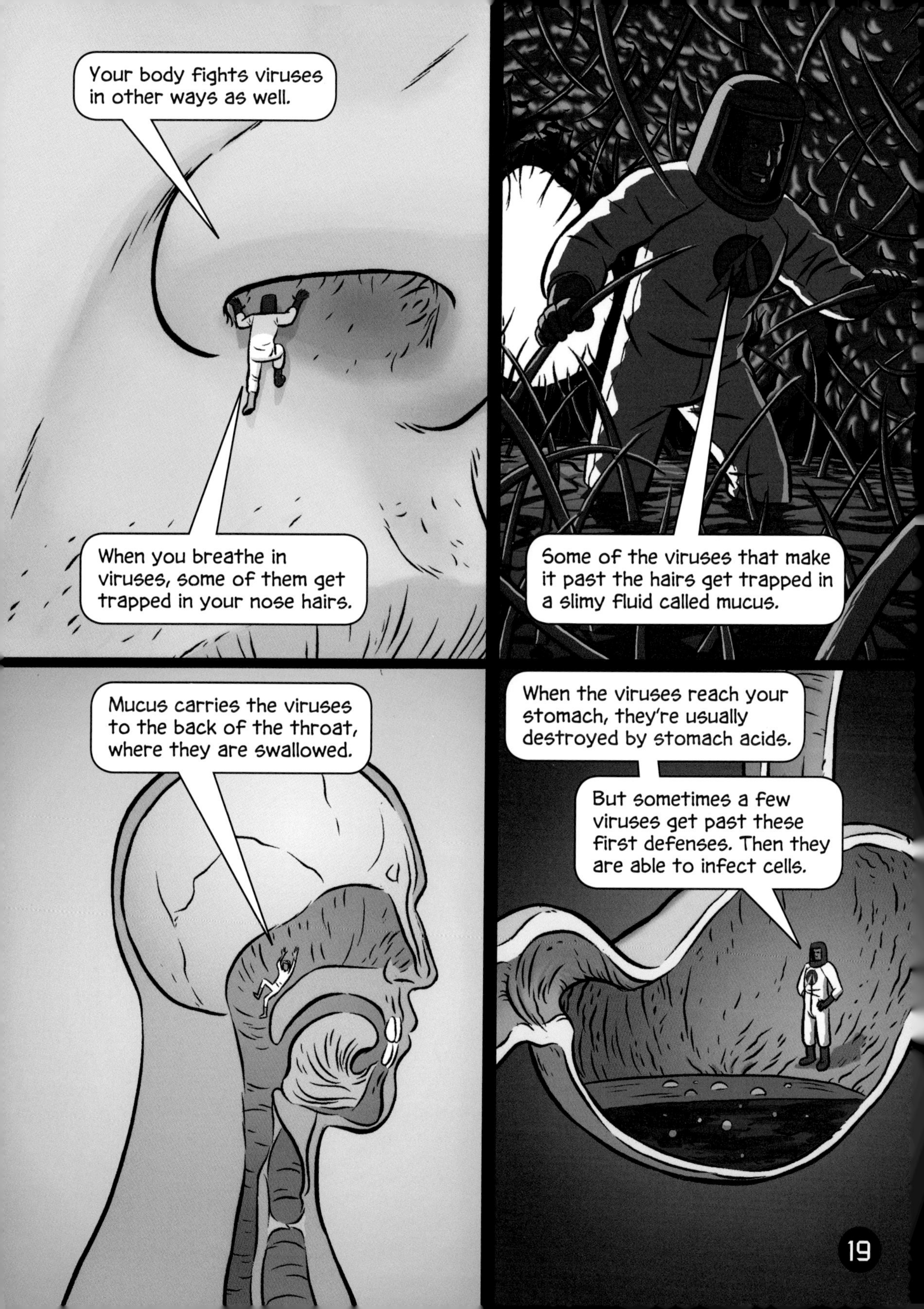

Your body fights viruses in other ways as well.

When you breathe in viruses, some of them get trapped in your nose hairs.

Some of the viruses that make it past the hairs get trapped in a slimy fluid called mucus.

Mucus carries the viruses to the back of the throat, where they are swallowed.

When the viruses reach your stomach, they're usually destroyed by stomach acids.

But sometimes a few viruses get past these first defenses. Then they are able to infect cells.

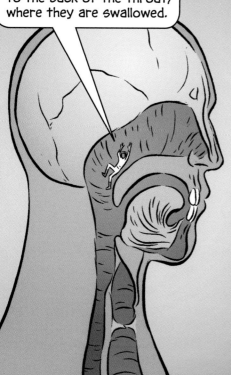

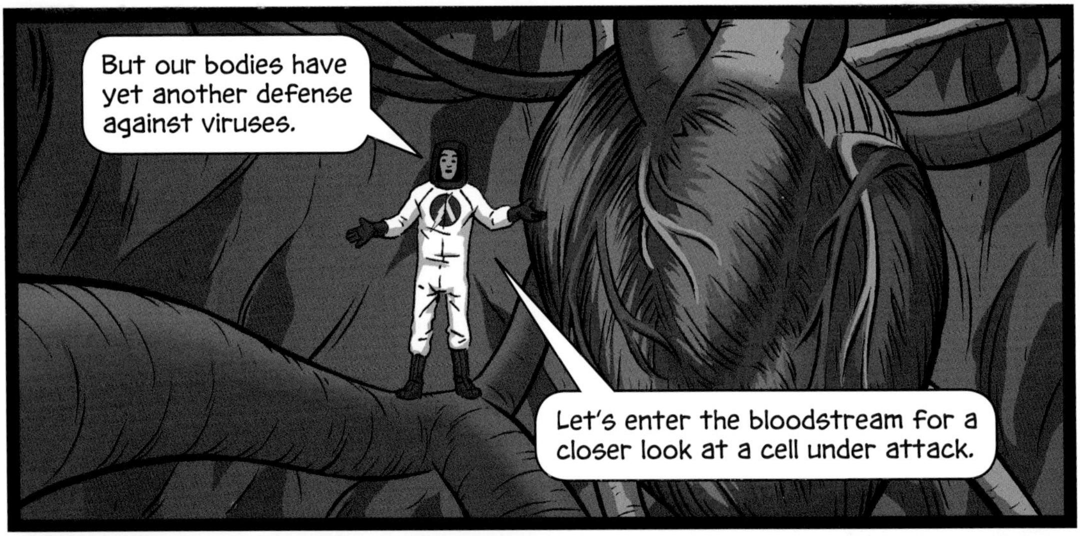
But our bodies have yet another defense against viruses.
Let's enter the bloodstream for a closer look at a cell under attack.

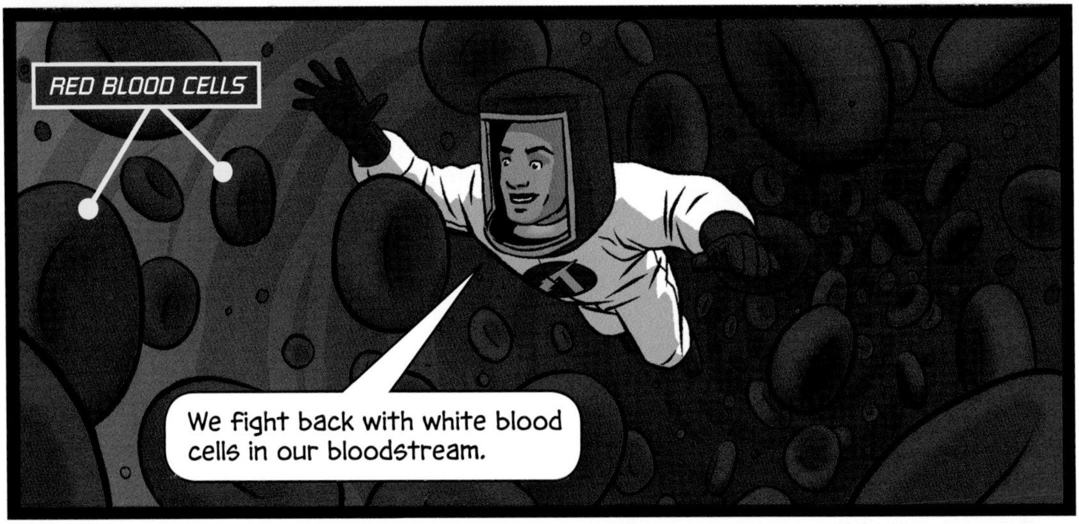
RED BLOOD CELLS
We fight back with white blood cells in our bloodstream.

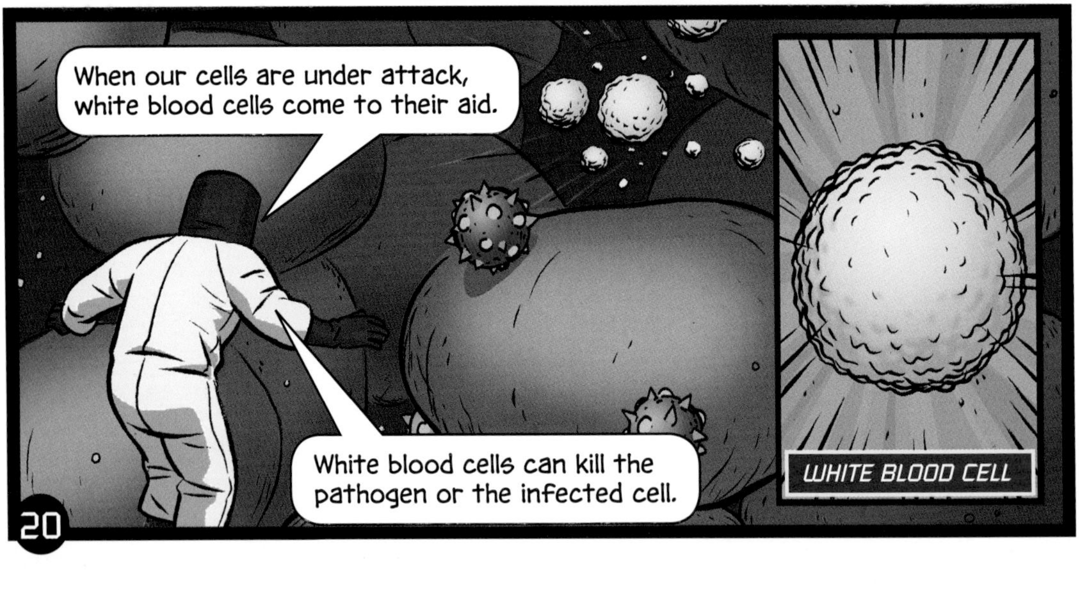
When our cells are under attack, white blood cells come to their aid.
White blood cells can kill the pathogen or the infected cell.
WHITE BLOOD CELL

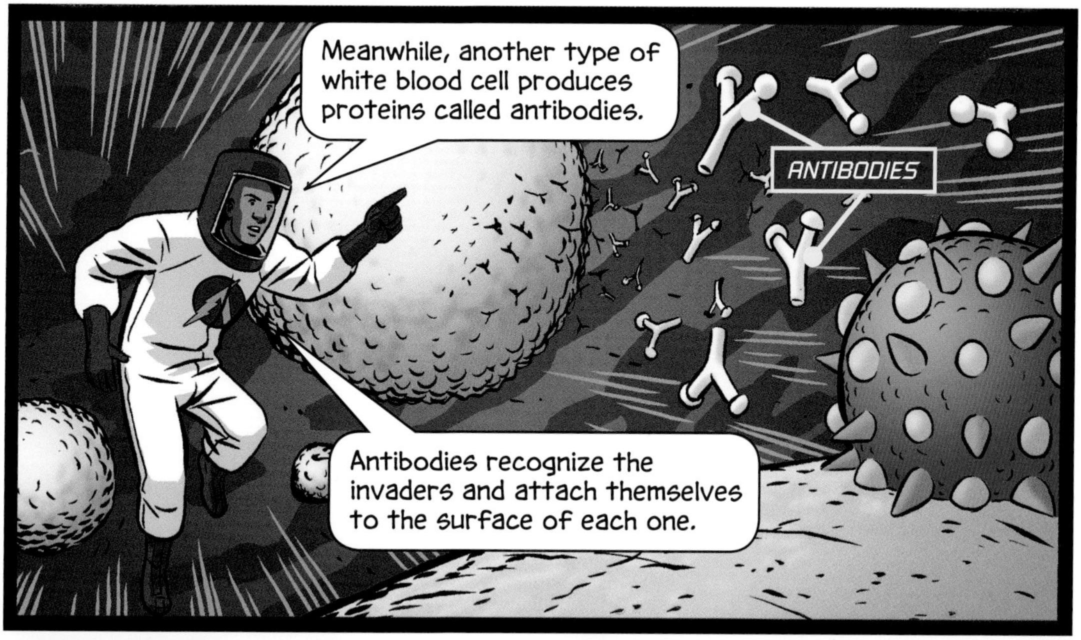
Meanwhile, another type of white blood cell produces proteins called antibodies.
ANTIBODIES
Antibodies recognize the invaders and attach themselves to the surface of each one.

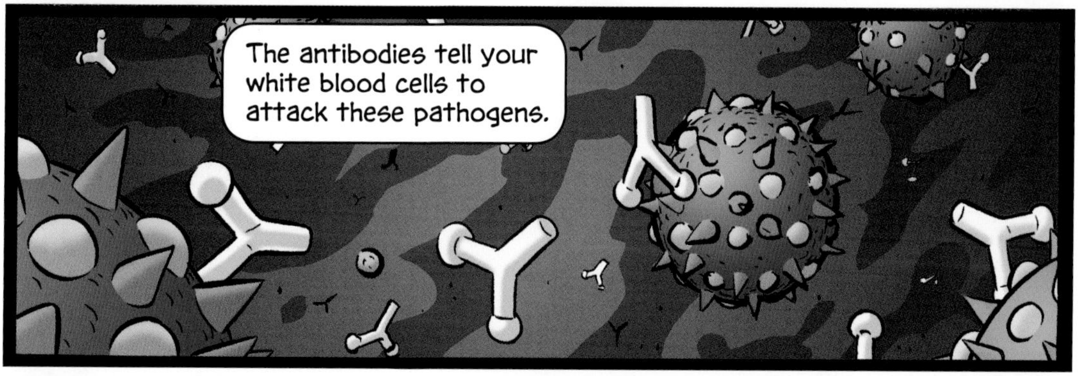
The antibodies tell your white blood cells to attack these pathogens.

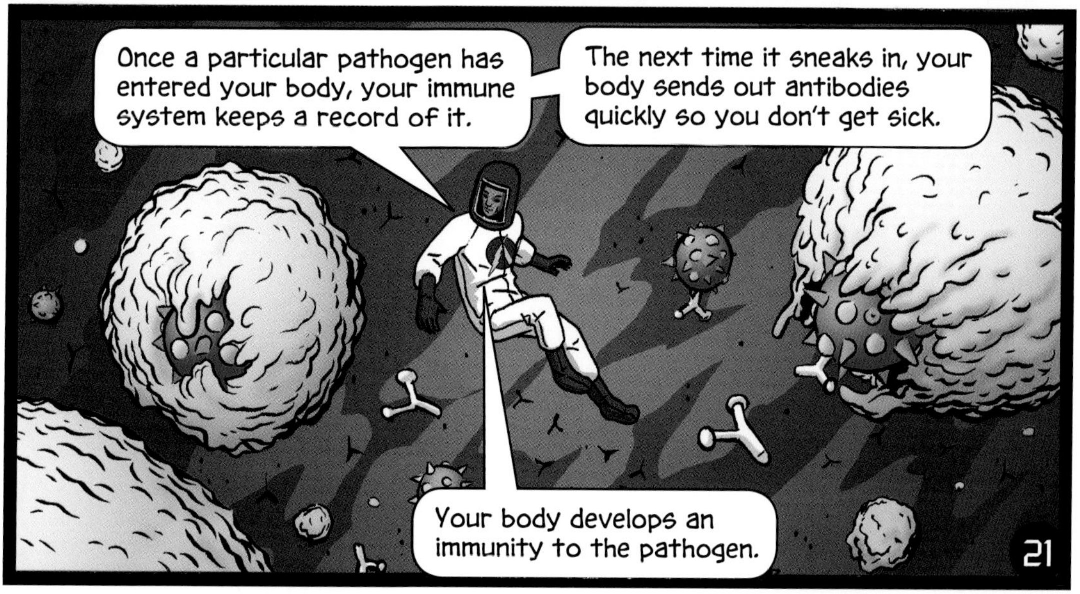
Once a particular pathogen has entered your body, your immune system keeps a record of it.
The next time it sneaks in, your body sends out antibodies quickly so you don't get sick.
Your body develops an immunity to the pathogen.

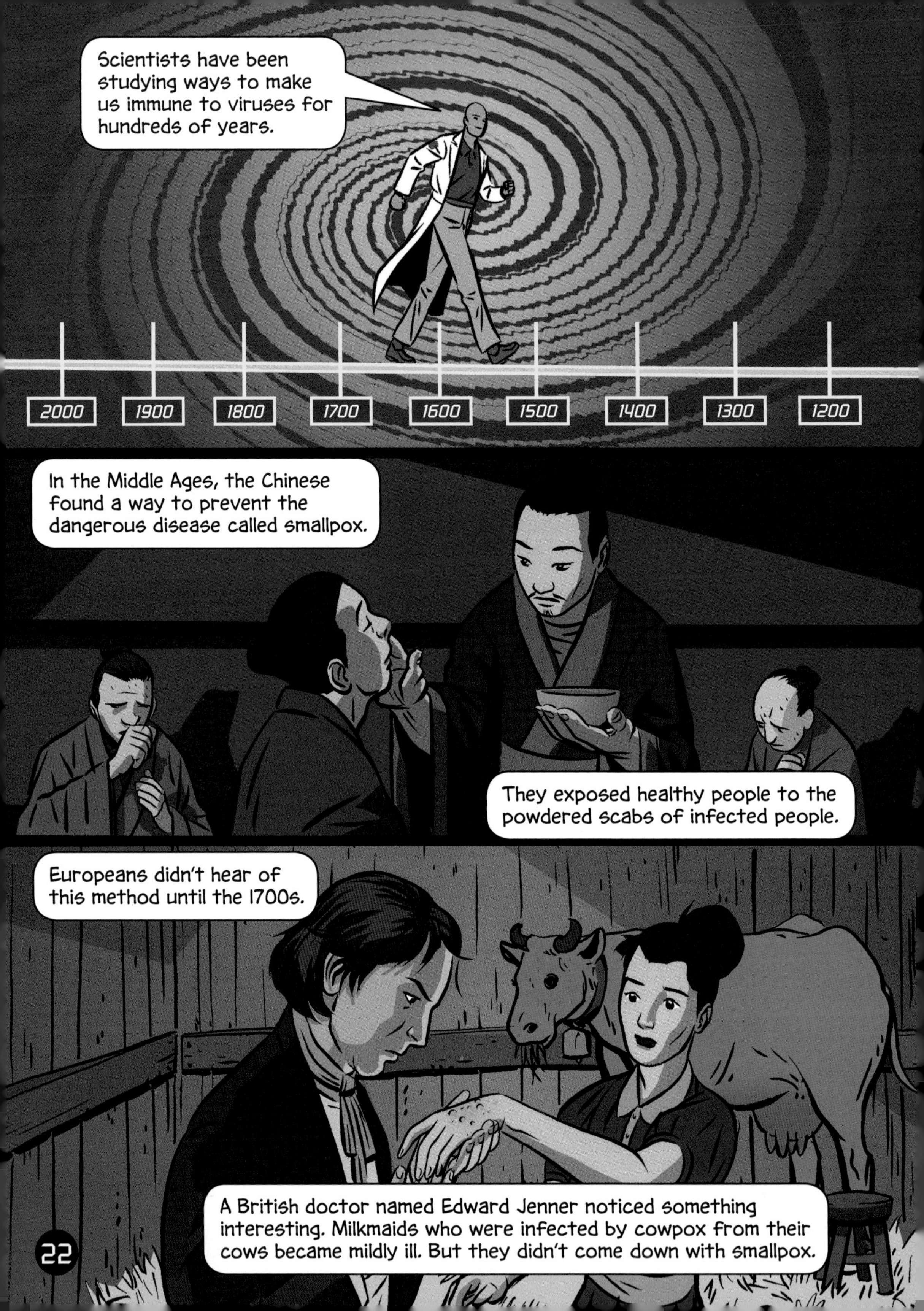
Scientists have been studying ways to make us immune to viruses for hundreds of years.
2000
1900
1800
1700
1600
1500
1400
1300
1200
In the Middle Ages, the Chinese found a way to prevent the dangerous disease called smallpox.
They exposed healthy people to the powdered scabs of infected people.
Europeans didn't hear of this method until the 1700s.
A British doctor named Edward Jenner noticed something interesting. Milkmaids who were infected by cowpox from their cows became mildly ill. But they didn't come down with smallpox.

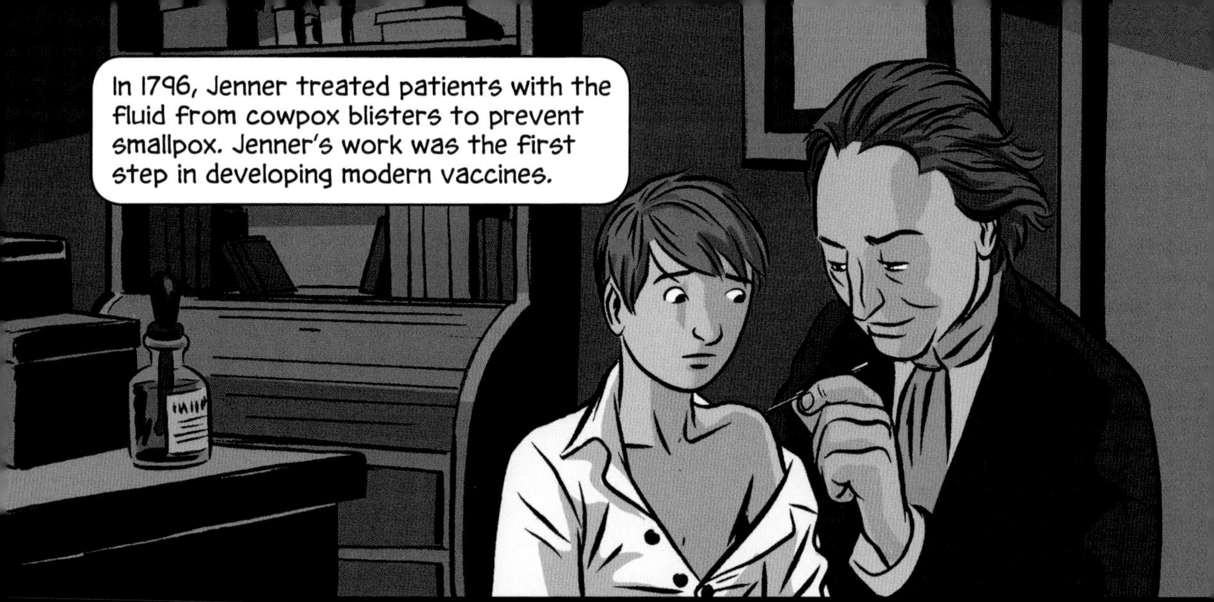
In 1796, Jenner treated patients with the fluid from cowpox blisters to prevent smallpox. Jenner's work was the first step in developing modern vaccines.

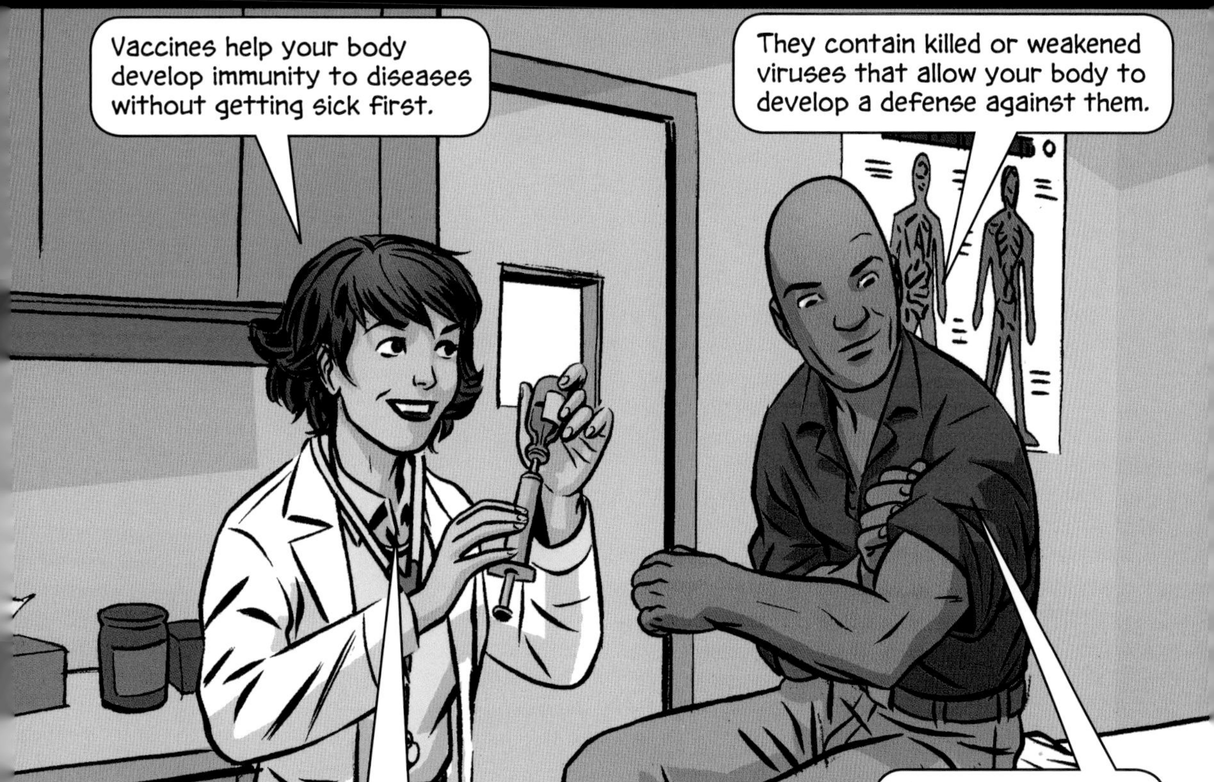
Vaccines help your body develop immunity to diseases without getting sick first.
They contain killed or weakened viruses that allow your body to develop a defense against them.
Vaccines prevent diseases like measles, mumps, and polio.
That's why you have to get your shots.

SMALLPOX

Thanks to vaccines, smallpox was officially removed from the world in 1980. But a few samples of the virus still exist in laboratories, under very heavy security.

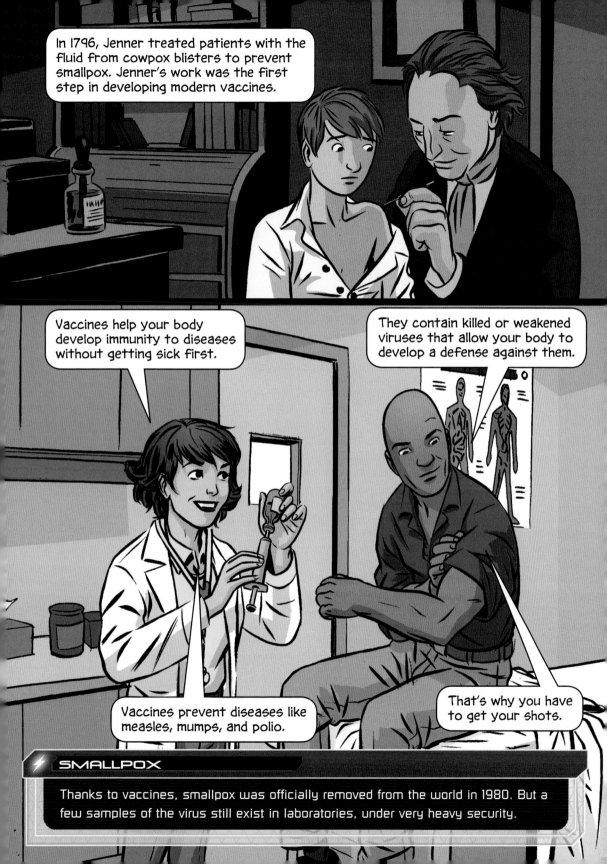

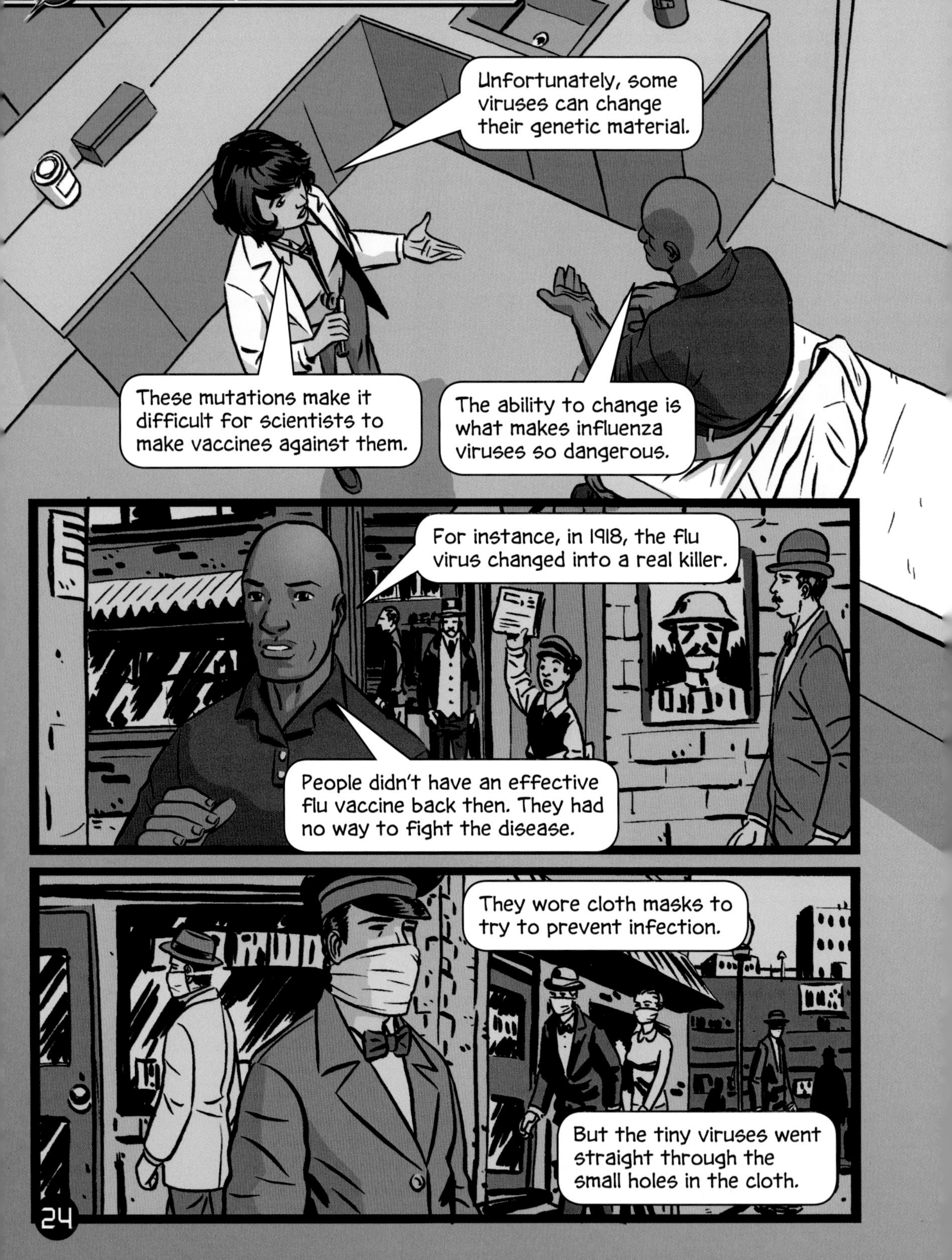
Unfortunately, some viruses can change their genetic material.
These mutations make it difficult for scientists to make vaccines against them.
The ability to change is what makes influenza viruses so dangerous.
For instance, in 1918, the flu virus changed into a real killer.
People didn't have an effective flu vaccine back then. They had no way to fight the disease.
They wore cloth masks to try to prevent infection.
But the tiny viruses went straight through the small holes in the cloth.

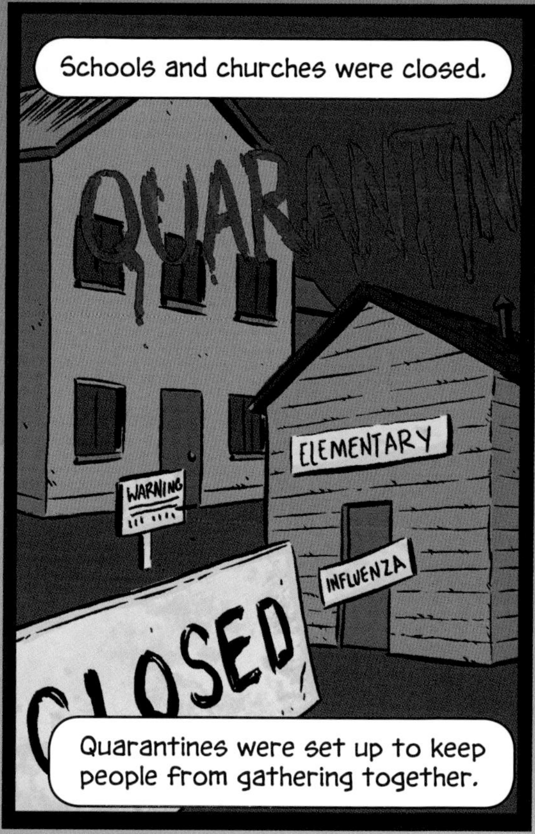
Schools and churches were closed.
QUAR
ELEMENTARY
WARNING
INFLUENZA
CLOSED
Quarantines were set up to keep people from gathering together.

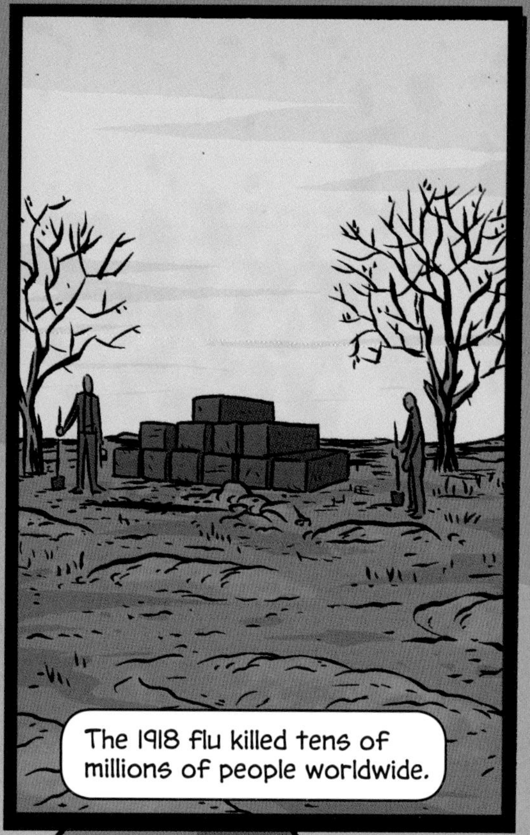
The 1918 flu killed tens of millions of people worldwide.

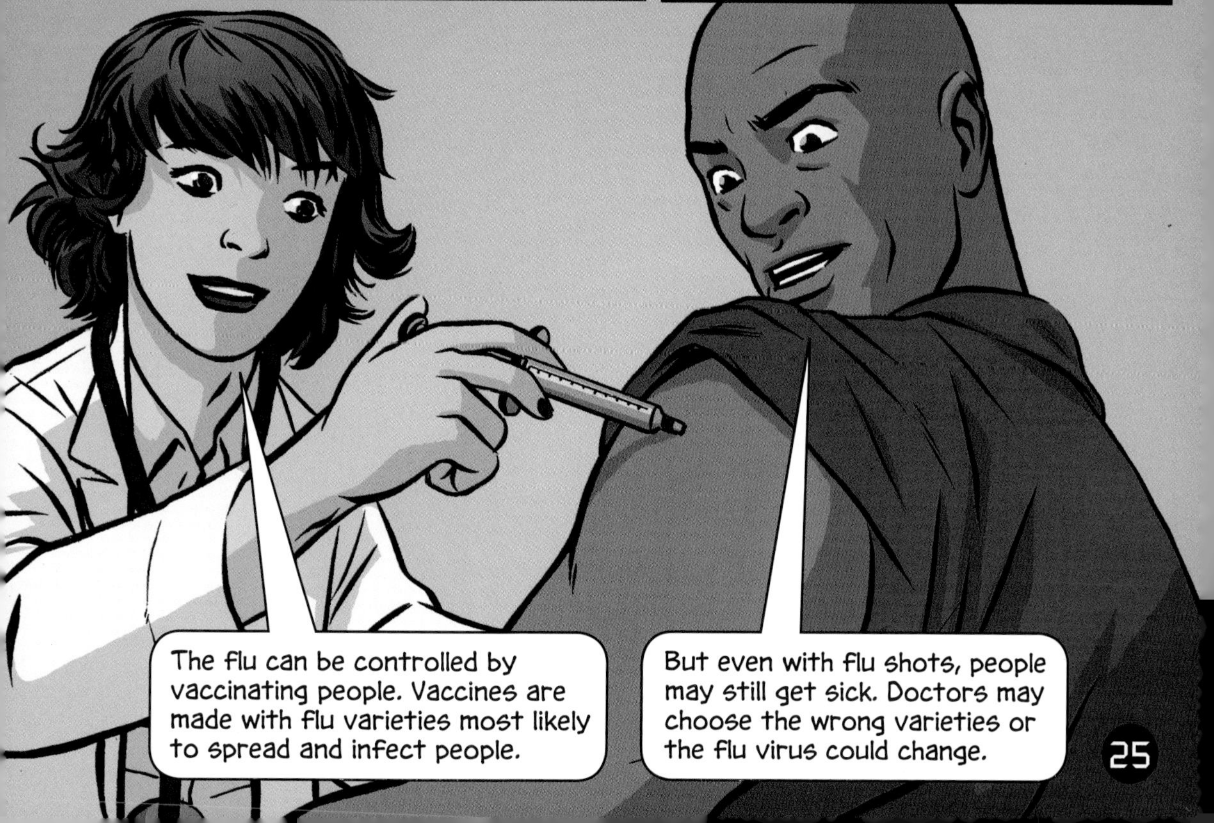
The flu can be controlled by vaccinating people. Vaccines are made with flu varieties most likely to spread and infect people.
But even with flu shots, people may still get sick. Doctors may choose the wrong varieties or the flu virus could change.

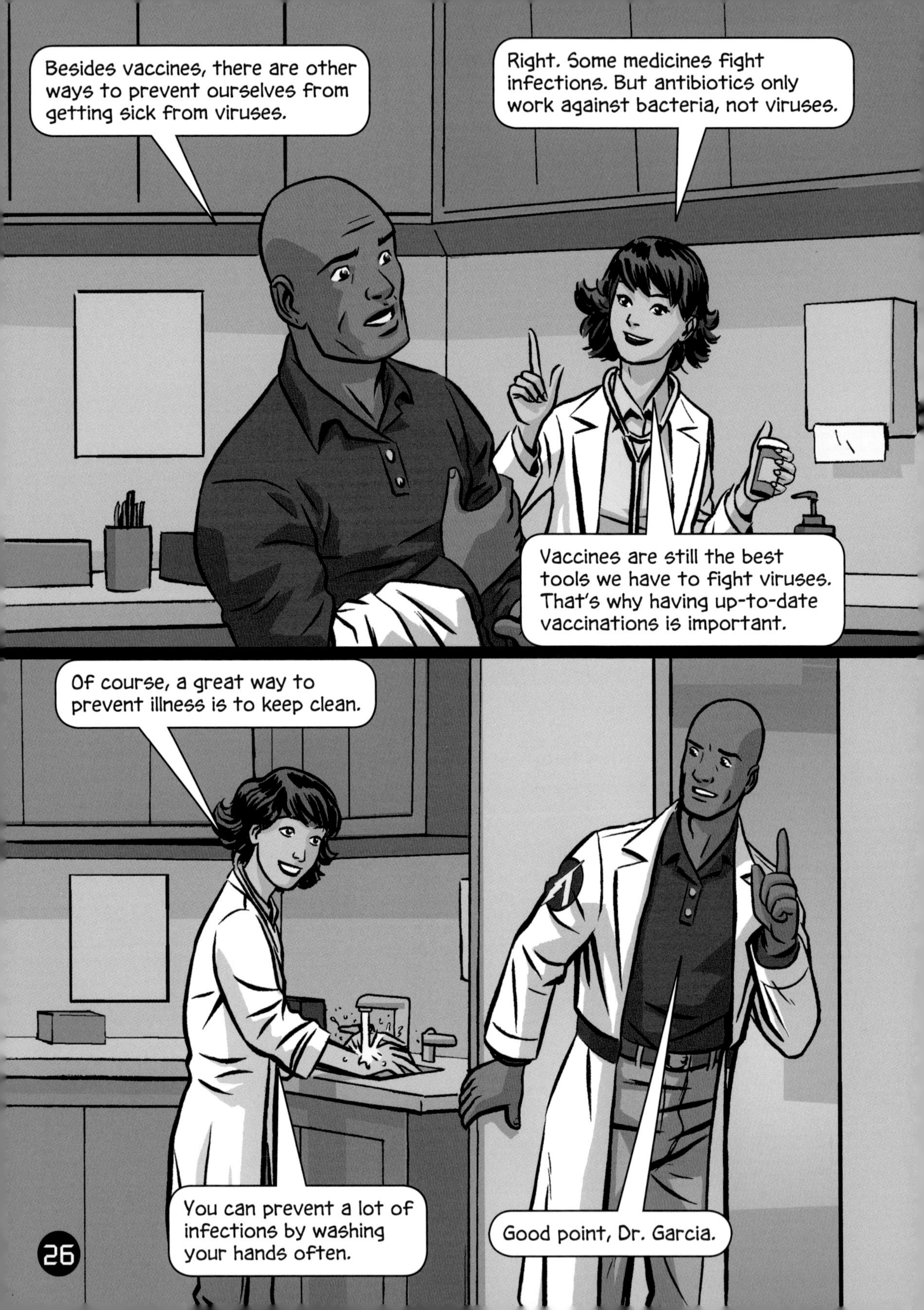

Besides vaccines, there are other ways to prevent ourselves from getting sick from viruses.
Right. Some medicines fight infections. But antibiotics only work against bacteria, not viruses.
Vaccines are still the best tools we have to fight viruses. That's why having up-to-date vaccinations is important.
Of course, a great way to prevent illness is to keep clean.
You can prevent a lot of infections by washing your hands often.
Good point, Dr. Garcia.

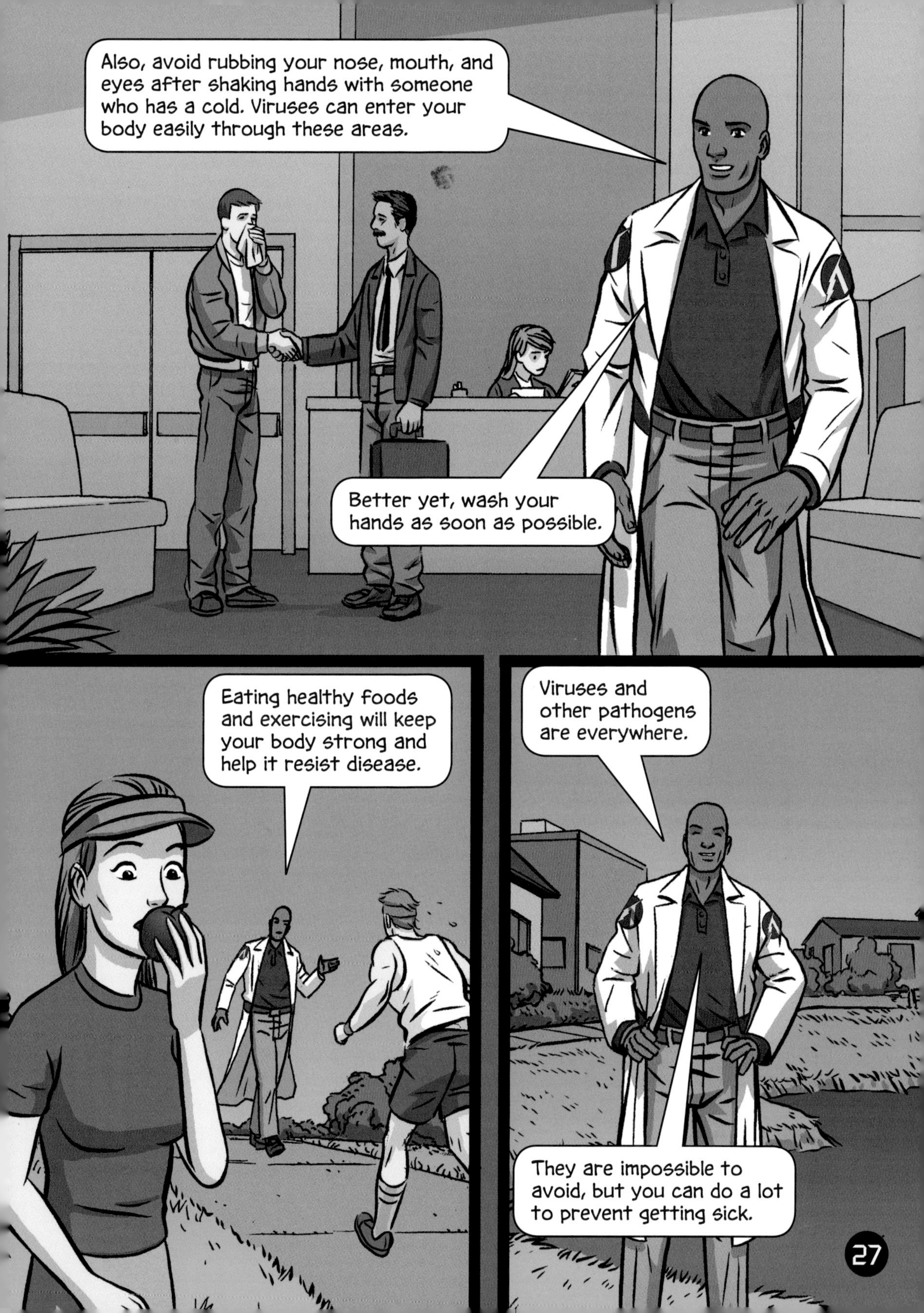
Also, avoid rubbing your nose, mouth, and eyes after shaking hands with someone who has a cold. Viruses can enter your body easily through these areas.
Better yet, wash your hands as soon as possible.
Eating healthy foods and exercising will keep your body strong and help it resist disease.
Viruses and other pathogens are everywhere.
They are impossible to avoid, but you can do a lot to prevent getting sick.

MORE ABOUT VIRUSES

We usually only hear about bad bacteria and ways to get rid of them. But only a small percentage of bacteria is truly harmful. In fact, many bacteria are very helpful. Without bacteria, we couldn't turn milk into cheese, sour cream, or yogurt. We use bacteria to help produce antibiotics and other medicines. Bacteria are even used to clean up oil spills.

Viruses can cause the colorful streaks and patterns you see in the petals of some tulips.

Having a fever is not always bad. Many viruses and bacteria don't grow as well when your body temperature rises above normal. A fever is often just your body trying to defend itself against infection.

Animals get sick from viruses too. That's why it's important to get your pets vaccinated against rabies, distemper, and other diseases.

Genetic mutations can sometimes allow a virus to jump from animals to humans. For example, pigs and birds can get the flu. In some cases, they can pass it on to people.

The virus known as HIV causes the serious disease called AIDS. HIV attacks the immune system, reducing its ability to fight off disease. HIV is spread only through direct contact with an infected person's bodily fluids, such as blood. Right now, there is no cure or vaccine for HIV infection or AIDS. Some medications, however, can help people with HIV live longer lives.

 Vaccines aren't just for viruses. They're also used to protect people against some diseases caused by bacteria. Scientists have made vaccines for bacteria such as diphtheria, pertussis (whooping cough), and tetanus.

 A computer virus is a computer program that copies itself. It is passed between computers like a virus is passed from person to person. And just like a regular virus, computer viruses can be harmful. They can delete data and steal personal information.

MORE ABOUT

MaxAxiom
SUPER SCIENTIST

Real name: Maxwell J. Axiom
Hometown: Seattle, Washington
Height: 6' 1"   **Weight:** 192 lbs
Eyes: Brown   **Hair:** None

Super capabilities: Super intelligence; able to shrink to the size of an atom; sunglasses give x-ray vision; lab coat allows for travel through time and space.

Origin: Since birth, Max Axiom seemed destined for greatness. His mother, a marine biologist, taught her son about the mysteries of the sea. His father, a nuclear physicist and volunteer park ranger, schooled Max on the wonders of earth and sky.

One day on a wilderness hike, a megacharged lightning bolt struck Max with blinding fury. When he awoke, Max discovered a newfound energy and set out to learn as much about science as possible. He traveled the globe earning degrees in every aspect of the field. Upon his return, he was ready to share his knowledge and new identity with the world. He had become Max Axiom, Super Scientist.

GLOSSARY

bacteria (bak-TIR-ee-uh) — one-celled, tiny organisms that can be found throughout nature; many bacteria are useful, but some cause disease.

DNA (dee-en-AY) — the molecule that carries all of the instructions to make a living thing and keep it working

HIV (AYCH-ie-vee) — the virus that causes AIDS; HIV attacks the body's immune system, making patients more likely to get other illnesses.

immune system (i-MYOON SISS-tuhm) — the part of the body that protects against germs and diseases

influenza (in-floo-EN-zuh) — an illness that is like a bad cold with fever and muscle pain; a virus causes influenza.

mutation (myoo-TAY-shuhn) — a permanent change in nature, form, or quality; when viruses mutate they sometimes become stronger and more dangerous.

pathogen (PATH-uh-juhn) — a germ that causes diseases

polio (POH-lee-oh) — an infectious viral disease that attacks the brain and spinal cord

quarantine (KWOR-uhn-teen) — limiting or forbidding the movement of people to prevent the spread of disease

RNA (AHR-en-ay) — a molecule found in all cells that carries instructions for making proteins

vaccine (vak-SEEN) — a substance used to protect people and animals against disease

READ MORE

Herbst, Judith. *Germ Theory.* Great Ideas of Science. Minneapolis: Twenty-First Century Books, 2008.

Kite, Patricia L. *Unicellular Organisms.* Sci-Hi Life Science. Chicago: Raintree, 2008.

Krohn, Katherine. *The 1918 Flu Pandemic.* Disasters in History. Mankato, Minn.: Capstone Press, 2008.

Nye, Bill. *Bill Nye the Science Guy's Great Big Book of Tiny Germs.* New York: Hyperion, 2005.

Snedden, Robert. *A World of Microorganisims.* Microlife. Chicago: Heinemann, 2007.

INTERNET SITES

FactHound offers a safe, fun way to find educator-approved Internet sites related to this book.

Here's what you do:

1. Visit *www.facthound.com*
2. Choose your grade level.
3. Begin your search.

This book's ID number is 9781429623384.

FactHound will fetch the best sites for you!

INDEX